PRAYING IN THE SPIRIT

Heavenly Resources
for
Praise and Intercession

Jack W. Ha̶̶̶̶̶
with
Rebecca B̶̶

THOMAS NELSON PUBLISHERS
Nashville • Atlanta • London • Vancouver

CONTENTS

Praying in the Spirit: Heavenly Resources for Praise and Intercession is one of a series of study guides that focus exciting, discovery-geared coverage of Bible book and power themes—all prompting dynamic, Holy Spirit-filled living.

About the Executive Editor

JACK W. HAYFORD, noted pastor, teacher, writer, and composer, is the Executive Editor of the complete series, working with the publisher in the conceiving and developing of each of the books.

Dr. Hayford is Senior Pastor of The Church On The Way, the First Foursquare Church of Van Nuys, California. He and his wife, Anna, have four married children, all of whom are active in either pastoral ministry or vital church life. As General Editor of the *Spirit-Filled Life Bible,* Pastor Hayford led a four-year project, which has resulted in the availability of one of today's most practical and popular study Bibles. He is author of more than twenty books, including *A Passion for Fullness, The Beauty of Spiritual Language, Rebuilding the Real You,* and *Prayer Is Invading the Impossible.* His musical compositions number over four hundred songs, including the widely sung "Majesty."

About the Writer

REBECCA HAYFORD BAUER is a housewife, mother, and writer, whose husband Scott is Executive Associate Pastor at The Church On The Way in Van Nuys, California. Besides serving as an editorial assistant to the Graphics Department at the church, a team she formerly led before motherly duties demanded more of her time, Becki is a writer in her own right and is recipient of the Gold Medallion Award for *The 25 Days of Christmas,* published by Victor Books in 1994. With her skills, she is often the key to the release of many books by her father, Pastor Jack Hayford.

She is a graduate of LIFE Bible College and has done post-graduate studies in writing at Pierce College in Los Angeles. Rebecca and Scott began their family just as he was completing study at Fuller Seminary, and they moved to Central California to take their first pastorate. They have three children: Brian, Kyle, and Lindsey.

Of this contributor, the Executive Editor has remarked: "It is heartwarming enough to see your daughter committed to Christ and the ministry, but all the more so because she is such a disciplined believer, devoted wife, diligent servant, and dedicated mother. She writes on family themes from a base of solid experience and genuine success as a wife and mom."

THE KEYS
THAT KEEP ON FREEING

And I will give you the keys of the kingdom of heaven, and whatever you bind on earth will be bound in heaven, and whatever you loose on earth will be loosed in heaven. (Matt. 16:19)

While there is no conclusive list of exactly what keys Jesus was referring to, it is clear that He did confer upon His church—upon *all* who believe—the access to a realm of spiritual partnership with Him in the dominion of His kingdom. The "keys" to this partnership are *concepts*—biblical themes that promote spiritual vitality when applied with faith under the lordship of Jesus Christ. The "partnership" is the *essential* feature of this release of divine grace; (1) believers reach to *receive* Christ's promise of "kingdom keys," (2) while choosing to *believe* in the Holy Spirit's readiness to unleash their power today.

Companions to the Bible book studies in the *Spirit-Filled Life Study Guide* series, the Kingdom Dynamic studies present a variety of different themes. This series is an outgrowth of the Kingdom Dynamics themes included throughout the *Spirit-Filled Life Bible*.

The central goal of this series of study guides is to help you discover "power points" of the Holy Spirit-filled life. Assisting you in your discoveries are a number of helpful features. Each study guide has twelve to fourteen lessons, each arranged so you can plumb the depths or skim the surface, depending upon your needs and interests. The study guides contain major lesson features, each marked by a symbol and heading for easy identification.

WORD WEALTH

The WORD WEALTH feature provides important definitions of key terms.

 ### BEHIND THE SCENES

BEHIND THE SCENES supplies information about cultural beliefs and practices, doctrinal disputes, business trades, and the like, that illuminate Bible passages and teachings.

 ### KINGDOM EXTRA

Because this study guide focuses on a theme of the Bible, you will find a KINGDOM EXTRA feature that guides you into Bible dictionaries, Bible encyclopedias, and other resources that will enable you to glean more from the Bible's wealth on the topic if you want something extra.

FAITH ALIVE

Finally, lessons contain FAITH ALIVE features. Here the focus is, So what? Given what the Bible says, what does it mean for my life? How can it impact my day-to-day needs, hurts, relationships, concerns, and whatever else is important to me? FAITH ALIVE will help you see and apply the practical relevance of God's literary gift.

As you'll see, these guides supply space for you to answer the study and life-application questions and exercises. You may, however, want to record all your answers, or just the overflow from your study or application, in a separate notebook or journal.

The Bible study method used in this series follows four basic steps. **Observation** answers the question, What does the text say? **Interpretation** deals with, What does the text mean?

—not to you or me, but what it meant to its original readers. **Correlation** asks, What light do other Scripture passages shed on this text? And **application,** the goal of Bible study, poses the question, How should my life change in response to the Holy Spirit's teaching of this text?

If you have used a Bible much before, you know that it comes in a variety of translations and paraphrases. Although you can use any of them with profit as you work through the *Spirit-Filled Life Kingdom Dynamics Study Guide* series, when Bible passages or words are cited, you will find they are from the *New King James Version* of the Bible. Using this translation with this series will make your study easier, but it's certainly not necessary.

A word of warning, though. By itself, Bible study will not transform your life. Through Bible study, you will grow in your understanding of the Lord, His kingdom and your place in it, and those things are essential. But you need more. You need to rely on the Holy Spirit to guide your study and your application of the Bible's truths. He, Jesus promised, was sent to teach us "all things" (John 14:26; cf. 1 Cor. 2:13). So as you use this series to guide you through Scripture, bathe your study time in prayer, asking the Spirit of God to illuminate the text, enlighten your mind, humble your will, and comfort your heart. He will never let you down. He promises you!

Lesson 1/Biblical Foundations of Spiritual Language

"My sister had spoken in tongues!

"She was the first one in our family to receive the baptism with the Holy Spirit and the evidence of spiritual language. But as happy as we were for her, the truth was, the rest of us felt something different than before—if not uncomfortable, at least uncertain.

"I sure felt that way.

"I wanted to ask her questions. But I didn't, because the questions in my mind sounded like funny things to ask a person; questions like 'How did you do it?' 'What does it feel like?' 'Do you know what you're saying?' 'Was it hard to start?'

"Further, I felt, well, somehow left out. My spiritual footings in Christ were secure enough that I knew I was *not* less saved than my sister now or less loved by God. Still, a low-grade sense of threat, bordering on rejection, began to creep into my soul. I felt neither jealousy toward my sister nor ingratitude nor irritation toward God. Rather, I simply had a peculiar sense of being on the outside of something that others were on the inside of. And as much as I was thankful for my sister's experience and joy, I still felt the question in my own soul: *Will it ever happen to me?*"[1]

The subject of spiritual language brings mixed responses from many and seems, somehow, shrouded in mystery—the "secret handshake" of the "truly blessed." For most of us, though, that "mystery" stems from our unfamiliarity with what Scripture says about spiritual language. Our understanding of spiritual language and our acquaintance with the Holy Spirit begins and ends in Acts 2, the day the Church was born through a powerful baptism with the Holy Spirit. But in actuality, spiritual language was prophesied long before the day of Pentecost arrived!

THE PERSON OF THE HOLY SPIRIT

Let's begin our study with an investigation of the Holy Spirit in Scripture. Look up the following Scriptures and write down the different ways that we see the Holy Spirit at work.

1 Samuel 16:13; Daniel 5:11

Psalm 51:12

Isaiah 59:19

Luke 4:18

John 6:63

John 14:16

 KINGDOM EXTRA

The Bible reveals that the Person of the Holy Spirit has been the primary agent in all of the ministry of the Word throughout the centuries. The Scripture states clearly that the triune Godhead operates coequally, coeternally, coexistently, as one unit. But it also has been suggested, and with validity, that we might view this unity of activity with an eye toward the special function of each member of the Trinity: the executive is the Father, the architect is the Son, and the contractor is the Holy Spirit.

Thus, the Holy Spirit, as contractor, anointed the Old Testament prophets Isaiah and Joel to write—to prophesy of the day when He would be outpoured and when His gifts would be exercised in the church, throughout the whole church age.[2]

John 16:7–11; Acts 10:19, 20; 16:6; Romans 8:14,15; 2 Corinthians 3:17; Ephesians 4:3; Hebrews 10:15; 2 Peter 1:20, 21

Further review of Scripture shows us specific ways that the Holy Spirit ministers to *us:*

Isaiah 11:2; 63:14; Zechariah 12:10; John 14:26; 16:13; Romans 8:26; Ephesians 1:17

FAITH ALIVE

Scripture gives many different names for the Holy Spirit (i.e., Rom. 8:15—the Spirit of adoption). Review the Scriptures above and write down one of the names of the Holy Spirit that applies to something you are currently facing.

TONGUES IN THE OLD TESTAMENT, TOO?

Now that we have an understanding of the person and ministry of the Holy Spirit in our lives, let's look at how the subject of tongues is introduced and understood throughout Scripture.

Look up the following verses and write down what they have to say about our tongues and the power of our speech.

Job 15:5

Psalm 5:9

Psalm 52:2

Psalm 109:2

When we lie, to whom are we submitting (John 8:44)?

To whom can we turn to seek freedom from lies (Ps. 120:2, 3)?

Proverbs 6 lists seven things that the Lord hates. What does it say about the tongue? (Prov. 6:16, 17)

Proverbs 15:1

Proverbs 17:27, 28

Proverbs 18:21

Proverbs 21:23

Proverbs 25:23

Compare Jeremiah 17:9 and Matthew 12:34. What do these verses add to our understanding about the words of our mouths?

James 1:26

James 3:6

James 3:8

Because of the unruliness of the tongue and our need to control it, it should come as no surprise that, in God's redemptive process, He has allowed "a new tongue" to be part of our inheritance. Not only does God promise to make us new from the inside out so that our speech becomes reflective of His life in us, He promises us a new language with which to commune with Him. The concept of "speaking to God in another language" is woven throughout Scripture. Look up the following verses and answer the questions.

How is the way we talk supposed to change once we have become one of the redeemed?

Psalm 16:8–11; Acts 2:26; Isaiah 35:6; Philippians 2:11; Colossians 4:6; James 4:11; Titus 3:2

What changed in Isaiah's speech as a result of his encounter with the Lord (Is. 6:5–8)?

A "multitude of languages" is first introduced in Genesis 11:1–9 at the Tower of Babel. Read this passage. Why do you think that God confused the language of the people?

Compare what was happening in the hearts of the people in Genesis 11 with what was happening in the hearts of those waiting on God in Acts 2:1. What do you think is the major difference between these two groups of people?

BEHIND THE SCENES

Noah's descendants reverted quickly to pagan ways, so the Lord decided to confuse their language and then scattered them. What they intended as a monument to human effort became a symbol of divine judgment on human pride and self-rule.

"Babel" is derived from the Hebrew *balal,* which means "mixed up" or "confused." The Babylonians later interpreted "Babel" to mean "the gate of the god." Most scholars link this city with Babylon, which eventually became synonymous with the final evil city that persecutes God's people (Rev. 17:18).[3]

Compare Isaiah 28:11 and 1 Corinthians 14:21, 22. What do these verses tell us about tongues?

KINGDOM EXTRA

In Isaiah 28:11, 12, God used Isaiah to tell Judah that He would teach them in a manner they did not like and that He would give them knowledge through the language of foreigners as a sign of their unbelief. Centuries later the apostle Paul expands the intent of this passage, referring it to the gift of speaking in tongues in the church as a manifestation or sign to unbelievers (1 Cor. 14:21, 22). This sign could be in languages either known or unknown to human beings (compare 1 Cor. 14 with Acts 2:1–11; 10:45, 46).[4]

While Joel did not specifically mention "tongues" in his prophecy about the pouring out of God's Spirit, Peter's sermon on the day of pentecost clearly links the prophecy to what was happening. Compare Joel 2:28–32 and Acts 2:14–21. How do you think tongues was a fulfillment of Joel's prophecy on the day of pentecost?

Ezekiel 39:29 also speaks of the outpouring of the Holy Spirit. Read Romans 11 and write down if you think the passage in Ezekiel applies to Gentiles as well as Israel, or just to Israel.

Copy Jesus' prophecy about spiritual language in Mark 16:17. If we ever feel uncertain about the biblical foundation of spiritual language, here we have the promise of it in our Savior's own words.

Read Jesus' post-Resurrection words to His disciples in John 20:19–23. Write down the commands Jesus gives His disciples in verses 21 and 22. Is there any significance in which command is listed first? What do you think that significance might be? Compare Jesus' breathing on the disciples in verse 22 with Genesis 2:7. What is happening in these two events? What is the significance of Jesus breathing on His disciples right before He establishes His Church? How do you think this event should affect your attitude toward receiving the Holy Spirit?

KINGDOM EXTRA

In John 20:22, the allusion to Genesis 2:7 is unmistakable. Now Jesus breathed life into His own. Some interpret the statement **Receive the Holy Spirit** as symbolic and as anticipating Pentecost. Others understand the Greek to denote immediacy in the sense of "receive right now," and view the day of the Lord's resurrection as marking the transition from the terms of the old covenant to those of the New Covenant. The old creation began with the breath of God; now the new creation begins with the breath of God the Son.[5]

SPIRITUAL LANGUAGE PRODUCES A LIFESTYLE

The early church understood that once the Holy Spirit swept through your life, it would never again be the same! Much of that understanding was related to the fact that the Greek and Hebrew words for spirit are also the same words used for breath. The first Christians knew that the presence of the spirit in their lives was their literal breath of life. On the day of pentecost, not only was the "breath" provided that made spiritual language possible, but the "spirit" that energized a whole lifestyle change was attendant as well. As an example, compare Peter on the night of Jesus' death (Luke 22:54–62) and on the day of pentecost (Acts 2:14–41). It is the presence of the Holy Spirit which also produces the fruits of a lifestyle filled with God's love and power. Galatians 5:22, 23 clearly declares that Holy Spirit fullness is more than merely language. It is also the fullness of the One who is changing us into the likeness of our Savior. Read the following Word Wealth, then write down how you think the presence of the Holy Spirit in your life might change *your* lifestyle.

 WORD WEALTH

In both Hebrew and Greek, the word for wind, breath, and spirit is the same word. *Ruach* (Hebrew) occurs nearly 400 times. Job 37:21 and Psalm 148:8 speak about "winds" related to storms. In Genesis 6:17, "the *ruach* of life" is translated "the breath of life." Generally *ruach* is translated "spirit," whether concerning the human spirit, a distressing spirit (1 Sam. 16:23), or the Spirit of God. The Holy Spirit is especially presented in Isaiah: God puts His Spirit upon the Messiah (42:1); He will pour out His Spirit upon Israel's descendants (44:3); Yahweh and His Spirit both send the Anointed One (48:16, a reference to the triune God); the Spirit of God commissions and empowers the Messiah (61:1–3).[6] In Greek, *pneuma* is that part of a person capable of responding to God. The Holy Spirit is the third person of the Trinity, who draws us to Christ, convicts us of sin, enables us to accept Christ as our personal Savior, assures us of salvation, and enables us to live the victorious life, understand the Bible, pray according to God's will, and share Christ with others. [7]

FAITH ALIVE

How has the presence of the Holy Spirit in your life changed your lifestyle?

How might it change in the future?

What areas of your life do you need to open to the Holy Spirit?

How do you think that the "wind" of the Holy Spirit has become your "breath of life"?

Look up these verses that tell us how we are to relate to the topic of being filled with the Spirit. Write down what our attitude is to be:

Ephesians 3:19

Ephesians 5:18

The tense of the Greek for *be filled* in Ephesians 5:18 makes clear that such a Spirit-filled condition does not stop with a single experience, but is maintained by "continually being filled."

What attitude toward spiritual language and its expression do these three verses authorize?

1 Corinthians 13:1; 14:18; 2 Timothy 1:7

The early church viewed the idea of Spirit-filled life with great joy and expectancy. Read the following verses on how that life manifested itself in the lives of the early Christians.

Acts 4:31; 13:52; Romans 15:14; 1 Corinthians 3:16

How might the following verses affect your daily choices?

Philippians 1:9–11

Colossians 1:9–12

Romans 8:6–9

Jude 20, 21

While the early church lived in Spirit-filled life, they understood that way of life to include speaking in tongues. Look up the following Scriptures and write down how many of the people spoke with tongues.

Acts 2:4

Acts 8:14–17

Acts 10:44

Acts 19:1–7

What was Paul's desire for believers in this regard?

1 Corinthians 14:5

Is this verse (and Paul's related desire for all believers) for us today? (See 2 Tim. 3:16, 17 and Heb. 13:8.)

As we continue through this study guide, we will be studying in depth the benefits of spiritual language in the life of the believer. Here, however, is a brief overview. Look up the following verses and write down how spiritual language is to be a resource to us.

John 16:13

Romans 8:26

Ephesians 6:14–18 (note verse 18)

Ephesians 5:19

1 Corinthians 14:4

There are also things that spiritual language is not to be in our lives. Read the Kingdom Extra below, then look up the verses following to see how we are to conduct our lives in the Spirit.

 KINGDOM EXTRA

Speaking with tongues is neither unbiblical nor outdated.

Speaking with tongues is not a transcendental experience.
Speaking with tongues is not a status symbol.
Speaking with tongues is not proposed as a substitute
for spiritual growth.[8]

1. Speaking with tongues is biblical: Acts 2:3, 4
2. Speaking with tongues is for today: Acts 2:38, 39
3. Speaking with tongues is not a transcendental experience, but the person speaking in tongues is in full control of
himself or herself: 1 Corinthians 14:32, 33, 40.
4. Speaking with tongues is not a status symbol. James
makes clear that we are never to favor one person above another.
Read James 2:1–9 and write down how this would influence our
actions toward others regardless of whether or not they have
spoken in tongues.
5. Speaking in tongues will aid our spiritual growth but
cannot substitute for it. John 16:5–15 discusses the work of the
Holy Spirit. Nowhere does John intimate that the presence of the
Spirit surrenders our involvement in spiritual life. Read this passage in John and write out what the Holy Spirit has come to do:

v. 7

vv. 8, 9

vv. 8, 10

vv. 8, 11

v. 13

v. 14

FAITH ALIVE

After studying the biblical foundation of spiritual language, what is your attitude toward the subject?

How is this like or unlike the attitude in the Scriptures you read?

In which area on this subject is the Lord inviting you to take a new step of faith by accepting a new outlook?

Write a prayer to the Lord about what you would like to see Him do in your heart as you explore the remainder of this study guide.

1. Jack Hayford, *The Beauty of Spiritual Language* (Dallas, TX: Word Publishing, 1992), 37–39.

2. *Spirit-Filled Life Bible* (Nashville, TN: Thomas Nelson Publishers, 1991), 2018–2019, "Holy Spirit Gifts and Power."

3. Ibid., 20–21, "Text notes on Genesis 11:5–8 and 11:9."

4. Ibid., 2018, 2019, "Holy Spirit Gifts and Power."

5. Ibid., 1613, "Text note on John 20:22."

6. Ibid., 474, "Word Wealth: 2 Sam. 23:2, Spirit."

7. Ibid., 1697, "Word Wealth: Rom. 7:6, Spirit."

8. Jack Hayford, *The Beauty of Spiritual Language* (Dallas, TX: Word Publishing, 1992), 21–22.

Lesson 2/The Purpose for Spiritual Language

Have you ever been in the uncomfortable position of being the person who "didn't get the joke"? That's how I felt the first time I went over to visit my husband's family! It was almost like they were speaking a different language, and I didn't get anything—the jokes, the comments, even what they called normal everyday household items! Families speak their own languages—an inside "familyspeak" that only they understand.

In certain respects, that is what spiritual language is between us and Father God. No matter what circumstance or situation we are in, we can reach out to the Father in prayer or praise, in desperation or weakness, silently or aloud—all through the vehicle of our spiritual language. Of course, we can also do that through "prayer with our understanding." But spiritual language is our "familyspeak" language, our Father tongue . . . a language just between you and Him.

Before we go on, let's review again several ways spiritual language is to be a resource to us. This, of course, isn't an exhaustive list but will help to focus our thinking on the basics.

John 14:16, 17; 16:13

Romans 8:26; Eph. 6:14–18

1 Corinthians 14:4

KINGDOM EXTRA

1. Speaking with tongues as the Holy Spirit gives utterance is the unique spiritual gift identified with the church of Jesus Christ. All other gifts, miracles, and spiritual manifestations were in evidence during Old Testament times, before the day of pentecost (Acts 2:1–39).

2. Speaking with tongues is a specific fulfillment of prophecies by Isaiah and Jesus. Compare Isaiah 28:11 with 1 Corinthians 14:21, and Mark 16:17 with Acts 2:4; 10:46; 19:6.

3. Speaking with tongues is an evidence of the baptism in or infilling of the Holy Spirit (Acts 2:4; 10:45, 46; 19:6).

4. Speaking with tongues is a spiritual gift for spiritual edification of the church when accompanied by interpretation (1 Cor. 14:5).

5. Speaking with tongues is a spiritual gift for communication with God in private worship (1 Cor. 14:15).

6. Speaking with tongues is a means by which the Holy Spirit intercedes through us in prayer (Rom. 8:26; 1 Cor. 14:14).

7. Speaking with tongues is a spiritual means for rejoicing (1 Cor. 14:15; Eph. 5:18, 19).

8. Paul's application of Isaiah's prophecy seems to indicate that speaking with tongues is also intended as a means of "rest" or "refreshing" (Is. 28:11, 12; 1 Cor. 14:21).

9. Tongues follow as one confirmation of the Word of God when it is preached (Mark 16:17, 20; 1 Cor. 14:22).[1]

As we look at the benefits of spiritual language in our lives, it is remarkable to see how every gift of God is so multi-faceted and complete to meet all of our needs. Copy below James 1:17.

What are the two words that describe God's gifts to us?

WORD WEALTH

Good, *agathos:* Good, in a physical and moral sense, and which produces benefits. The word is used of persons, things, acts, conditions, and so on. A synonym of *agathos* is *kalos,* good in an esthetic sense, suggesting attractiveness, excellence.[2] Perfect, *teleios:* From *telos,* "end." *Teleios* refers to that which has reached an end, that is, finished, complete, perfect. When applied to persons, it signifies consummate soundness, and includes the idea of being whole.[3]

The lists of the benefits of spiritual language we've looked at so far can be categorized into four basic groups: 1) expanded worship, 2) enabled warfare, 3) edification of the believer, and 4) communication with the Father. We will look at these one at a time, but first let's take a look at how these four features manifested themselves in the early church.

BEHIND THE SCENES

Luke 24:49 tells us Jesus' last command to His disciples, "tarry in the city . . . until you are endued with power from on high." Luke picks up the sequence of events in the Book of Acts with Jesus' promise, "But you shall receive power when the Holy Spirit has come upon you" (Acts 1:8).

As commanded, the disciples waited in Jerusalem: "These all continued with one accord in prayer and supplication" (Acts 1:14). But the fact is, they had no idea what they were waiting for! They just knew that the Lord had promised them "Holy Spirit power."

After the outpouring of the Holy Spirit, however, as we read through the Book of Acts, we see the disciples functioning in the same life of the Spirit that is promised to us today. See the disciples as they move in expanded worship (2:47; 5:41), enabled warfare (16:16–26; 19:19), edification of the believer (4:32; 9:31), and communication with the Father (4:24–31; 6:4). And best of all, all of this is available to us today, "For the promise is to you and to your children, and to all who are afar off, as many as the Lord our God will call" (Acts 2:39).

EXPANDED WORSHIP

Worship is at the very core of life in the kingdom of God. The story of Scripture begins and ends with worship. Job (Job 38:4–7) tells us that at creation "the sons of God shouted for

joy." Creation took place in the midst of the angelic choir praising the Almighty. And the Book of Revelation tells of the people
of God joining that choir in eternal praise around the throne of
God (Rev. 5:9–14). In between is a thread woven throughout
Scripture of God seeking a people to worship Him with all of
their hearts.

 KINGDOM EXTRA

First Peter 2:9 not only appoints praise, but represents <u>a
basic revelation of the Bible:</u> God wants a people who will
walk with Him in prayer, march with Him in praise, and thank
and worship Him. Note the progression in Peter's description
of the people of the New Covenant: 1) <u>We are a chosen gen-
eration</u>—a people begun with Jesus' choice of the Twelve,
who became 120, to whom were added thousands at Pentecost. We are a part of this continually expanding generation,
"chosen" when we receive Christ. 2) <u>We are a royal priesthood.</u> Under the Old Covenant the priesthood and royalty
were separated. We are now—in the Person of our Lord—all
"kings and priests to His God" (Rev. 1:6), a worshiping host
and a kingly band, prepared for walking with Him in the light
or warring beside Him against the hosts of darkness. 3) <u>We
are a holy nation,</u> composed of Jews and Gentiles—of one
blood, from every nation under heaven. 4) <u>We are His own
special people.</u> God's intention from the time of Abraham has
been to call forth a people with a special mission—to proclaim
His praise and to propagate His blessing throughout the
Earth.[4]

Look up these verses on worship and write down what you
learn about how we are to live our lives in worship to the Most
High.

Genesis 22:5
(Read the entire account of Abraham's devotion in worship.
What lessons stand out to you?)

Exodus 20:3–6

1 Samuel 15:25

2 Samuel 6:14

2 Samuel 24:24

Psalm 22:3, 4

Psalm 63:1–5

Psalm 150:1–6

Isaiah 27:13

Isaiah 66:23

Zephaniah 2:11

Matthew 21:16

John 4:23

Romans 12:1

Philippians 3:3

Hebrews 13:10–15

WORD WEALTH

Praise and worship are concepts mentioned throughout Scripture, but few understand their difference and the place for both in the lives of believers.

In the Old Testament Hebrew, *halal* means to praise, to thank; rejoice, or boast about someone. *Halal* is the root from which "hallellujah" is formed (literally, "all of you must praise Jah"). Also derived from *halal* is *tehillah,* or *tehillim* in the plural. A *tehillah* is a praise, a psalm, or a song. *Halal* conveys the idea of speaking or singing about the glories, virtues, or honor of someone or something.[5] In the Greek New Testament, *epainos* means approbation, commendation, approval, praise. *Epainos* expresses not only praise for what God does for us, but also for who He is, recognizing His glory.[6]

Worship carries a much different meaning, however. The Hebrew word, *shachah,* and the Greek word, *proskuneo,* carry similar meanings. *Shachah* means to bow, to stoop; to bow down before someone as an act of submission or reverence; to worship; to fall or bow down when paying homage to God. The primary meaning is "to make oneself low."[7] *Proskuneo* comes from *pros,* "toward," and *kuneo,* "to kiss," and carries the idea of prostrating oneself in worship, to bow down, do obeisance, show reverence, do homage, worship, adore. In the New Testament the word especially denotes homage rendered to God and the ascended Christ. All believers have a one-dimensional worship, to the only Lord and Savior. We do not worship angels, saints, shrines, relics, or religious personages.[8]

To see how spiritual language helps expand our capacity to worship the Lord, let's compare the band of disciples before and after the outpouring of the Holy Spirit in Acts 2.

Following the resurrection, what were the disciples' responses?

Matthew 28:17; Mark 16:11–13; Luke 24:17, 24:36, 37; John 21:3 (Compare to Matthew 4:18–20.)

By the time we reach the Book of Acts, the disciples were beginning to understand that Jesus had a mission for them. What was their reaction now?

Acts 1:4

Acts 1:6 (What does this verse tell us about the understanding the disciples had of what Jesus was setting before them?)

Acts 1:9–11

Acts 1:14

Acts 1:15–24

Look at Jesus' final commands to and commissioning of His disciples. Before the Acts 2 outpouring of the Holy Spirit, were the disciples fulfilling these commands?
Matthew 28:18–20

Mark 16:15–18 (See also vv. 19, 20. Were the disciples ministering in this way yet?)

Luke 24:44–49 (See also vv. 50–53.)

Now let's look at this band of disciples after Acts 2. Write down how they have changed and how you think spiritual language affected their capacity for praise.

Acts 2:11

Acts 2:46, 47

Acts 5:41

Acts 16:25

2 Corinthians 6:4, 10

1 Thessalonians 2:19

ENABLED WARFARE

The warfare of the Spirit will be covered in depth in Lesson Nine.

EDIFICATION

Spiritual language can be used for self-edification as well as for edification of others. Look up the following verses and write down if they direct personal edification or the building up of others.

Romans 14:19

1 Corinthians 14:4

1 Corinthians 14:5, 12

1 Corinthians 14:26

Ephesians 2:21

Ephesians 4:16

Jude 20

These Scriptures are fairly evenly divided between edifying yourself, edifying others, and Jesus edifying His church. Do you think it is all right to seek after self-edification? Why or why not?

If it's in the Bible, it must have some importance. What do you think that importance may be?

Look up these Scriptures on how the Lord strengthens us. Does this change how you view edifying yourself?

Psalm 27:14; 138:3; Ephesians 3:16; Philippians 4:13; Colossians 1:10, 11; 2 Timothy 4:17

How do you think edifying yourself affects your ability to minister to others?

Look up these verses and list the different ways these Scriptures say that we can minister to and build up the lives of others.

Mark 10:43, 44

John 12:26

John 13:14

Romans 14:21

1 Corinthians 10:24

Ephesians 5:19

Galatians 6:2, 10

Philippians 2:4

WORD WEALTH

The word translated "edify" is *oikodomeo,* and literally means "to be a house-builder." It stems, however, from two other Greek words: *oikos,* which means "a dwelling," and, by implication, "a family"; and *doma,* meaning "an edifice."[9]

Based on the preceding Word Wealth, read the following Scriptures and write down how the concepts of "family" and "house-building" apply to the church.

Isaiah 28:16

Matthew 16:18

1 Corinthians 3:11, 16

Galatians 6:10

Ephesians 2:19–22

1 Peter 2:5

 FAITH ALIVE

Look up and write down Proverbs 14:1. (Men—don't be put off by the fact that this verse appears to be written only to women. As the Bride of Christ, this verse can apply to all of us.)

List ways that you have been building up your "house" by edifying yourself.

What ways have you been tearing down your house?

List ways that you have been building up the house of God by edifying those around you.

What ways can you edify others even more?

Stop and pray that the Lord will help you as you grow in Him and bless those around you. Also present to Him any areas where you feel that you are "tearing down your house" and ask Him to help you eliminate those from your life.

COMMUNICATION WITH THE FATHER

Our communication with the Father takes place through prayer. Let's begin looking at the effect of prayer in our lives by looking at the Lord's Prayer (Matt. 6:9–13). As you read, write down how this prayer is an example for us in format, attitude, and subject.

KINGDOM EXTRA

The Lord's Prayer is a prayer outline with seven major topics, each representing a basic human need: 1) <u>The Paternal Need: "Our Father" (v. 9)</u>. When you pray, all needs are met by the benevolence of a loving Father. 2) <u>God's Presence: "Hallowed be Your name" (v. 9)</u>. Enter His presence through praise (Ps. 100:4), and call Him "Father" because of Christ's atoning blood (Heb. 10:19–22; Gal. 4:4–6). 3) <u>God's Priorities: "Your kingdom come" (v. 10)</u>. Declare that His kingdom priorities (Rom. 14:17) shall be established in yourself, your loved ones, your church, and your nation. 4) <u>God's Provision: "Give us" (v. 11)</u>. Jesus, the need-meeter, told us to pray daily, asking Him to supply all our needs. 5) <u>God's Forgiveness: "And forgive us" (v. 12)</u>. You need God's forgiveness, and you need to forgive others. Daily set your will to walk in love and forgiveness. 6) <u>Power Over Satan: And "do not lead us . . . deliver us from the evil one" (v. 13)</u>. Pray a hedge of protection about yourself and your loved ones (Job 1:9, 10; Ps. 91), and verbally put on the armor of God (Eph. 6:14–18). 7) <u>Divine Partnership: "For Yours is the kingdom" v. 13)</u>. Praise God for sharing His kingdom, power, and glory with you (2 Tim. 4:18; Luke 10:19; John 17:22). This is the prayer that teaches you how to pray.[10]

Look up the following Scriptures and write down which of the seven basic human needs listed above each corresponds to. The first one has been done for you.

Exodus 33:15—God's   Psalm 36:8
   presence

Psalm 103:3   Isaiah 43:2

Isaiah 64:8	Zechariah 4:6
Malachi 3:10	Matthew 6:33
Matthew 28:20	Mark 12:29, 30
Luke 6:38	John 1:12
Acts 5:31	Romans 8:15, 16
Romans 8:17	2 Corinthians 6:18
Galatians 4:6	Ephesians 1:7
Ephesians 3:19	Ephesians 6:12
Philippians 4:19	1 Timothy 2:1, 2
Hebrews 13:5	James 1:27

1 Peter 3:22—Who is this verse talking about?

Compare 1 Peter 3:22 to Ephesians 1:20–22. *Where* did God put all principalities?

Now, in the context of those two Scriptures, read Ephesians 2:6. Where has God seated us?

Where does that put all "principalities and powers and mights and dominions" in relation to us?

1 John 1:9

1 John 2:13

Revelation 12:11

WORD WEALTH

Pray, *proseuchomai:* The word is progressive. Starting
with the noun, *euche,* which is a prayer to God that also
includes making a vow, the word expands to the verb
euchomai, a special term describing an invocation, request,
or entreaty. Adding *pros,* "in the direction of" (God), *proseuchomai* becomes the most frequent word for prayer.[11]

Now, let's look at some of the things the apostle Paul said
about prayer. As you look up these verses, write down how spiritual language assists us in prayer.

1 Corinthians 14:2

1 Corinthians 14:14

What does Paul encourage us to do in 1 Corinthians 14:15?

Ephesians 6:18

How might spiritual language make Paul's command in
1 Thessalonians 5:17 possible?

Look at 1 Corinthians 14:18. What was Paul thankful for?

Why do you think he expressed thankfulness for that? What do you think he would have viewed as the benefit of "speak[ing] with tongues more than you all"?

Read the account of Jesus' life in John 4:1–38 referenced above. Can you find similarities in Jesus' and the apostle Paul's dependence upon and fulfillment in prayer? Write them down.

Scripture repeatedly speaks of Jesus setting aside time for prayer. Look up the following Scriptures to see our Lord at prayer.

Matthew 11:25; Mark 1:35; 6:46, 47; Luke 3:21; 5:15, 16; 6:12; 9:18; 22:41, 42; John 11:41; 17:1

 FAITH ALIVE

If Jesus needed to spend considerable amounts of time in prayer, we need to that much more! Look again at the pattern our Lord taught us to pray in the Lord's Prayer.

Which of the "seven basic human needs" we discussed in relation to the Lord's Prayer do you need right now?

Review again the Scriptures we discussed on that topic, and ask the Lord to begin to meet that need in your life.

How much time do you spend in "prayer with your understanding" each day?

How much time do you spend in "prayer in the Spirit" each day?

If you do not do this daily, covenant with the Lord right now to begin a time of communion with Him in prayer.

1. *Spirit-Filled Life Bible* (Nashville, TN: Thomas Nelson Publishers, 1991), 2020–2021, "Tongues for Personal Edification."

2. Ibid., 1802, "Word Wealth: Phil. 1:6, good."

3. Ibid., 1898–1899, "Word Wealth: James 3:2, perfect."

4. Ibid., 1910, "Kingdom Dynamics: 1 Pet. 2:9, Worshipful Walk with God."

5. Ibid., 599, "Word Wealth: 1 Chr. 23:30, praise."

6. Ibid., 1787, "Word Wealth: Eph. 1:6, praise."

7. Ibid., 838, "Word Wealth: Psalm 99:5, worship."

8. Ibid., 1967, "Word Wealth: Rev. 4:10, worship."

9. James Strong, *The New Strong's Exhaustive Concordance of the Bible:* Greek Dictionary of the New Testament (Nashville, TN: Thomas Nelson, 1995), #1430, 3618, 3624.

10. *Spirit-Filled Life Bible* (Nashville, TN: Thomas Nelson Publishers, 1991), 1414–1415, Kingdom Dynamics: Matt. 6:9–13, "The Lord's Prayer."

11. Ibid., 1414, "Word Wealth: Matt. 6:6, pray."

Lesson 3/How to Be Baptized with the Holy Spirit

There are as many accounts as there are individuals when it comes to people experiencing Holy Spirit baptism. Some are dynamic and miraculous, some are quite ordinary, others are the result of laborious seeking after God. Just within our own family there is quite a diversity.

My own personal pursuit of Holy Spirit baptism took place over a six-month period of time. Faithfully, after every service in church I sought prayer, and I tried and I tried. In retrospect I'm sure that was the problem. The filling of the Holy Spirit is a gift, not an effort. I needed to receive what the Father had for me and not fight to lay hold of it. Finally, I spoke with my earthly father (he's my pastor, too). He thought that I might be trying too hard, and he asked me a simple question. "Are there any words that you feel inside that just have not yet come out?" I replied, "Yes!" And when I spoke those two words I realized that it was truly the beginning of my prayer language in tongues and I began to use this language.

For my husband it was a similar circumstance. He sought after his spiritual language for two years. Finally, and quite uneventfully, he began in spiritual language on the 405 Freeway in bumper-to-bumper traffic while on his way to U.C.L.A. one January morning.

However, for my two sons it was radically different. They were baptized in water as fifth and sixth graders, and as they came out from beneath the water and began to praise God, they were powerfully, dramatically, and supernaturally launched into their prayer language. They felt the power of God rush through them, and they spoke in their new language for forty-five minutes without stopping. When asked about the experience, they both remarked how surprised they were with the overwhelming nature of this experience.

Which way is correct? How does the Holy Spirit deal differently with each personality? Why is it so easy for some and so difficult for others to receive?

What Do I Do To Be Baptized With The Holy Spirit?

Part of the problem for most people when seeking the baptism with the Holy Spirit comes from the question, "What do I do?" On the one hand the question is misplaced. *We* don't do anything. It is the Holy Spirit who gives us the language, and it is Jesus Himself who is the baptizer (see John 1:33). On the other hand, it is the absence of doing that keeps some from being able to receive. True, Jesus is the baptizer with the Holy Spirit. True, the Holy Spirit is the one who gives the language. But, we are the ones who *choose to speak* what the Holy Spirit gives us. So, "What do I do?" becomes the crucial question in receiving your spiritual language.

Read Luke 11:9–13 and answer the questions below.

In verse 9, what are we supposed to do?

Why did Jesus give this parable?

Who is being contrasted with earthly fathers in verse 13?

Why did Jesus talk about good earthly fathers?

What does Jesus promise to those who "ask" the Heavenly Father?

What are "good gifts" related to in verse 13?

How do you receive a gift from God?

One of the problems with "What do I do?" presumes that the baptism with the Holy Spirit is related to a level of spiritual attainment. People struggle with receiving a prayer language because they do not feel "holy enough."

What does Acts 2:38 say concerning the Holy Spirit? Why is it called the "gift" of the Holy Spirit? How do you receive a gift from God?

Read James 1:6, 7. How do we approach the Lord to receive His gifts in verse 6? Is it possible to receive anything from God without faith?

Look again at Acts 2:38. When does a believer receive this "gift of the Holy Spirit"? According to Peter does this "gift" follow salvation?

One of the great difficulties of the theology of the baptism with the Holy Spirit relates to *when* a person receives the Holy Spirit and *what* the difference is between the experience of receiving the Holy Spirit and Holy Spirit baptism. In Lesson Four this issue is discussed in detail. For now, let's review these principles:

1. A person receives the Holy Spirit at salvation, just as the disciples did in John 20:23 when Jesus breathed on them. It is a certainty that faith in Jesus Christ, as our Lord and Savior, guarantees the Holy Spirit's presence in our life (Rom. 8:9–17).

2. A person receives the baptism with the Holy Spirit following conversion as an act of faith (Acts 2:38) for the empowering of our ministry.

THE PRESENCE AND POWER OF THE HOLY SPIRIT

Acts 8 gives us an example in the early church of a group of believers in Samaria who had already accepted Jesus as their Savior, but who had yet to receive the baptism with the Holy Spirit. Read Acts 8 and then answer the questions below.

Were the Samaritans believers in Christ before John and Peter arrived?

What does verse 12 tell us about their spiritual condition?

According to Romans 10:9, 10 were these believers who were baptized (v. 12) Christians?

Since they were believers, did they possess the Holy Spirit?

Why then did Peter and John lay hands on them in verse 17?

Throughout the Gospels and Acts there is an expectation of a baptism whereby a person acknowledges their sinfulness and the regenerating power of Jesus Christ in their life by faith (Mark 16:16; Acts 22:16). Here the Holy Spirit enters a person's life by faith and makes him or her part of the acknowledged community of believers at baptism.

  KINGDOM EXTRA

Peter calls upon his audience to change their opinion of and attitude toward Christ and **to be baptized in the name of Jesus Christ** as a public acknowledgment that they had accepted Jesus as Messiah and Lord. "Name" suggested nature or character; therefore, to be baptized "in the name of Jesus" is to confess Him to be all that His name denotes. Baptism in and of itself is not a means of forgiveness and salvation (see 3:19). For the early church, however, there was no separation between ritual and reality. Coming to Christ and being baptized were mutually inclusive.[1]

In addition, the Gospels and Acts describe a second experience of the Holy Spirit empowering the individual for service. Read Luke 3:16. Who is the baptizer with the Holy Spirit?

What does Luke teach regarding a difference between water and Holy Spirit baptism?

Is water baptism necessary for every believer (Mark 16:16)?

Read Matthew 3:13. Who baptized Jesus in water?

According to verse 15, why was Jesus baptized?

What followed Jesus' baptism in water? The Holy Spirit of God was seen "alighting upon Him." What does that mean?

How did Jesus' life change after the Holy Spirit came upon Him?

What was the heavenly Father's response in verse 17?

What did Jesus do to be baptized in water?

What did Jesus do to receive the Holy Spirit?

How Did the Early Church Receive Holy Spirit Baptism?

Some people feel that Jesus provides a model that none could ever follow. The reality of Immanuel, God with us in Jesus, places Him in a special category. He may be completely human, but He is also completely divine. However, studying how the early church was baptized with the Holy Spirit puts us on solid ground for our own personal pursuit.

⚔ WORD WEALTH

"With one accord," *homothumadon:* Being unanimous, having mutual consent, being in agreement, having group unity, having one mind, and purpose. The disciples had an intellectual unanimity, and emotional rapport, and volitional agreement in the newly founded church. In each of its occurrences, *homothumadon* shows a harmony leading to action.[2]

Read Acts 2:4 again. What did the Holy Spirit do? As a result, what did the 120 do in this verse?

Who spoke? Who gave the language?

Read Acts 8:14–17. What did Peter and John do?

Do you think that Peter and John may have also instructed those in Samaria concerning 1) the things that had happened in Jerusalem and 2) the baptism with the Holy Spirit?

Why did Peter and John lay hands on them?

What happened as a result in verse 17?

Read Acts 9:17, 18. Why did Ananias call Saul "brother"?

What did Ananias do to Saul? What did Saul do?

Ananias was sent to Saul for two reasons. What were they in verse 17?

What happened when Ananias laid hands on Saul in verse 18? (Irrespective of "when" he began speaking in tongues, what do we *know* of Paul and spiritual language? 1 Cor. 14:18.)

Read Acts 10:44–47. What did Peter do in verse 44?

How many of the Gentiles experienced the Holy Spirit who "fell upon them"?

According to verse 45 what was received by these Gentiles?

What did the Gentiles do in response to the experience with the Holy Spirit in verse 46?

Why were Peter's companions "astonished" in verse 45?

What resulted after they received the gift of the Holy Spirit, according to verses 47, 48?

Read Acts 19:1–6. What was Paul's concern in verse 2?

Why did Paul rebaptize the people at Ephesus? Why did Paul lay hands on those who were baptized in the name of the Lord Jesus?

What did the people do after hands were laid on them in verse 6?

How do verse 2 and verse 6 go together in this passage?

By Way of Summary

Holy Spirit baptism occurs after salvation. It is here that the person is "filled with the Holy Spirit." This is different from and in addition to the entry into a person's life of the Holy Spirit at conversion. This Holy Spirit baptism is:
- Described with a number of different phrases;
- Can manifest itself in a number of different ways;
- Can be ministered in a number of ways.

Let's review the five instances of those who were baptized with the Holy Spirit in Acts.

Acts 2:4   Description: "filled with the Holy Spirit"
                 Manifestation: Wind, Fire, Tongues
                 Manner of ministry: They were gathered together
                 Who received: ALL

Acts 8:17   Description: "they received the Holy Spirit"
                 Manifestation: miraculous but not stated
                 Manner of ministry: laying on of hands
                 Who received: believers in Samaria

Acts 9:17   Description: "filled with the Holy Spirit"
                 Manifestation: delivered from blindness
                 Manner of ministry: laying on of hands
                 Who received: Saul

Acts 10:44–46   Description: "The Holy Spirit fell"
                 "the gift of the Holy Spirit poured out"
                 Manifestation: Tongues
                 Manner of ministry: Preaching
                 Who received: ALL

Acts 19:6   Description: "the Holy Spirit came upon them"
                 Manifestation: Tongues and Prophecy
                 Manner of ministry: laying on of hands
                 Who received: All twelve

In each account of Holy Spirit baptism in the Book of Acts, as people are prayed for or ministered to, they receive Holy Spirit fullness. Regardless of the stated manifestation at the time of Holy Spirit baptism, one thing is very clear: all present receive the gift of the Holy Spirit by faith and this results in a miracle sign. This sign is manifested in three out of five cases with the exercise of spiritual language. In the other two cases without the mention of tongues, one is the apostle Paul, whom we know spoke with tongues, and the other was in Samaria, where there was an unstated miracle sign. Clearly, the expectation of the early church was that spiritual language was normal and was related to being filled with the Holy Spirit. Those who were filled simply spoke "as the Spirit gave them utterance."

Since the fullness of the Holy Spirit is received by faith and is not related at all to spiritual maturity or attainment, we must break the misconception that receiving spiritual language is proof of Christian superiority. However, spiritual language does offer access in prayer and praise which can only be beneficial to the ongoing development in our walk with Christ (1 Cor. 14:2–4, 15).

 FAITH ALIVE

Have you been born again? The person who is going to be filled with the Spirit must have the indwelling Spirit and must belong to Jesus (Rom. 8:9).

Read 1 Corinthians 12:13. *By whom* are we "baptized into one body?"

Read Romans 6:3. According to this passage, into what are we baptized?

Have you been baptized with the Holy Spirit?

If you have not yet been baptized with the Holy Spirit, answer these questions which outline basic essential steps to being baptized with the Holy Spirit.

Have you asked? The Bible says, if we ask for the Holy Spirit, that prayer will be answered (Luke 11:8).

Have you surrendered? The apostle Paul made this need clear in the Book of Romans when he said, "Present your bodies a living sacrifice" (Rom 12:1).

Are you willing to obey the Spirit? God does not give this power to someone and then say, "You can take the part you like and leave the part you do not like." If you want to be immersed in the Holy Spirit, you need to be prepared to obey the Spirit (Acts 5:32).

Do you believe that you *will* receive? The apostle Paul said, "Did you receive the Spirit by the works of the law, or by the hearing of faith?" (Gal. 3:2). The answer, obviously, is faith. You have to believe that if you ask, you will receive.

Finally, you have to exercise what God has given you. Having asked, having received, having been willing to obey, and having believed, you need to respond in a biblical fashion. The Bible says those baptized with the Holy Spirit on the day of pentecost "began to speak with other tongues, as the Spirit gave them utterance" (Acts 2:4). This means they spoke the words that the Spirit gave them. The Holy Spirit gave the words, but the apostles and disciples voluntarily responded. There was action based on faith, not merely passive acceptance of the blessing. That is the way it is with God. God is offering the baptism in the Holy Spirit to people who need only to reach out and take it and then enjoy the blessing.[3]

A Prayer for Inviting the Lord to Fill You with the Holy Spirit

Dear Lord Jesus,
    I thank You and praise You for Your great love and faithfulness to me.

My heart is filled with joy whenever I think of the great gift
of salvation You have so freely given to me,
  And I humbly glorify You, Lord Jesus,
    for You have forgiven me all my sins and brought me to
      the Father.
  Now I come in obedience to Your call.
  I want to receive the fullness of the Holy Spirit.
  I do not come because I am worthy myself, but because
You have invited me to come.
  Because You have washed me from my sins,
    I thank You that You have made the vessel of my life a
      worthy one to be filled with the Holy Spirit of God.
  I want to be overflowed with Your life,
    Your love and Your power, Lord Jesus.
  I want to show forth Your grace,
    Your words,
      Your goodness, and
        Your gifts.
  to everyone I can.
  And so with simple, childlike faith, I ask You, Lord,
    Fill me with the Holy Spirit.
    I open all of myself to You,
      to receive all of Yourself in me.
  I love You, Lord, and I lift my voice in praise to You.
  I welcome Your might and Your miracles
    to be manifested in me
        for Your glory
        and unto Your praise.

I don't tell people to say amen at the end of this prayer,
because after inviting Jesus to fill you, it is good to begin to
praise Him in faith. Praisefully worship Jesus and simply allow
the Holy Spirit to help you do so. He will manifest Himself in a
Christ-glorifying way, and you can ask Him to enrich this
moment by causing you to know the presence and power of the
Lord Jesus. Don't hesitate to expect the same things in your
experience as occurred to people in the Bible. The spirit of
praise is an appropriate way to express that expectation, and to
make Jesus your focus, worship as you praise. Glorify Him and
leave the rest to the Holy Spirit.[4]

1. *Spirit-Filled Life Bible* (Nashville, TN: Thomas Nelson Publishers, 1991), 1628, "Text note on Acts 2:38."

2. *Spirit-Filled Life Bible,* 1624, "Word Wealth: Acts 2:1, with one accord."

3. Ibid., 1998, "Spiritual Answers to Hard Questions: How do I receive the baptism in the Holy Spirit?"

4. Jack Hayford, *The Beauty of Spiritual Language* (Dallas, TX: Word Publishing Co. 1992), 189–190.

Lesson 4/Spirit Baptism and "Initial Evidence"

Jenny made a discovery in the first six months of her marriage to Steve: some words didn't carry the same meanings to the two of them. They had a particularly difficult time with the word "maybe." Whenever the word was used in a decision-making situation they wound up with hurt feelings at best, or angry words at worst.

For Steve, "maybe" was simply a delay tactic. It meant, "Let's put off making a decision until later when it will either be too late to do anything about it or 'maybe' the person will forget the subject altogether." For him, it was the kindest way he could think of to benignly kill an idea. When Jenny used the word "maybe" it meant exactly that—"Maybe, I will try my hardest and see if I can make this happen."

One day, Jenny had mentioned that she would like to go out to a movie. With both of them still in college as well as carrying full-time job responsibilities, "maybe" was a fair response to her desire. The conflict came later that day when it became apparent that Steve had completely disregarded the issue, while Jenny had spent the entire morning working at top speed so everything would be finished and they could go out.

After several months of these kinds of miscommunications, Steve and Jenny realized that what had begun as a different understanding of the same word was becoming an issue of division between them. So they spent some time redefining "maybe" for use in their newly established home. They found that coming to terms with the use of that word has made life considerably easier—now that they both agree on a definition and both use it the same way.

THE DEBATE OVER "INITIAL EVIDENCE"

That is the case in the body of Christ over the phrase "initial evidence" (which, by the way, is not a biblical term). In traditional Pentecostal circles this term is used concerning the personal experience of spiritual language in a believer's life. The problem with the phrase is in its theological application. "The initial evidence" refers to the experience of the baptism with the Holy Spirit. In traditional Pentecostal theology *the only* acceptable evidence of Spirit-baptism is tongues.

This creates a theological and practical problem for many. First, those who are unfamiliar with Pentecostal theology presume that the absence of Holy Spirit baptism means that a person does not have the presence of the Holy Spirit in their life without speaking in tongues. These people rightly believe that they received the Holy Spirit at conversion.

Read John 3:1–8 and answer the questions below.

How is a person born again (3:5, 6)?

What must a person do to be born again (3:16–18)?

Read Romans 8:9–17. According to verse 9, what must *every believer* possess?

If we are "born of the Spirit," as in John 3:6, what dwells within us according to Romans 8:11?

How do we know that we are born again according to Romans 8:16?

The second problem many people have with the phrase "initial evidence" is that they may have had profound experiences with the Holy Spirit in which they began to function in the gifts of the Holy Spirit *before* they spoke with tongues. These people object to the "evidence" of Spirit baptism being restricted to the matter of speaking in tongues when there are nine gifts of the Holy Spirit listed in 1 Corinthians 12.

Read 1 Corinthians 12:3–11, and answer the following questions.

What enables a person to declare, "Jesus is Lord"?

What do gifts (v.4), ministries (v.5), and works (v.6) all have in common?

List the nine "gifts" ("manifestations" v. 7) of the Spirit in verses 8–10?

How are these "gifts" distributed in the body of Christ?

WHAT IS THE BAPTISM WITH THE HOLY SPIRIT?

It may help us in this study to have an agreed-upon definition of what the baptism with the Holy Spirit entails.

Read John 1:29–34. What did John the Baptist have to say concerning the baptism with the Holy Spirit?

How many baptisms are talked about in this passage?

What is the difference between water baptism and the baptism with the Holy Spirit in this passage?

List the three different phrases used for Jesus in verses 22, 24, 29.

Who is the one baptizing with water?

Who will baptize with the Holy Spirit?

There are other references in the Gospels to Jesus' role as "baptizer." Read the following verses.
Matthew 3:11
Mark 1:8
Luke 3:16
The verses in Matthew and Luke add to our understanding of Jesus' role of baptizer. What is it?

We know that Luke the physician wrote both the Gospel of Luke and Acts. One of the instructions given the disciples just before the Ascension is found in Luke 24:49, and repeated in Acts 1:4. What is that instruction?

In Luke 24:49 the phrase "the Promise of My Father," and in Acts 1:4 "the Promise of the Father" are used. What does this refer to?

In Acts 1:5 Jesus promises that they will be "baptized with the Holy Spirit not many days from now." What event is Jesus referring to?

In Acts 1:8 Jesus promises, "you shall receive power when the Holy Spirit has come upon you. . . ." Is this the same as the promise of the baptism with the Holy Spirit referred to in 1:5?

Read Acts 2:1–4.
Is this "the Promise of the Father" in Acts 1:4?

Is this the fulfillment of "you shall be baptized with the Holy Spirit" in Acts 1:5?

Is this the coming of the "power" of the Holy Spirit as prophesied by Jesus in Acts 1:8?

 KINGDOM EXTRA

As Jesus presented post-Resurrection teaching "pertaining to the kingdom of God" (v. 3), His disciples asked if now—with the Cross behind—the ultimate messianic kingdom would come. "It is not yours to know the future," He says, "but it is yours to receive the Spirit's power!" With those words, He makes three points: 1) The Holy Spirit is the Person and the Power by which assistance and ability are given for serving, for sharing the life and power of God's kingdom with others. 2) The Holy Spirit's power must be "received"; it is not an automatic experience. As surely as the Holy Spirit indwells each believer (Rom. 8:9), so surely will He fill and overflow (John 7:37–39) each who receives the Holy Spirit in childlike faith. 3) When the Holy Spirit fills you, you will know it. Jesus said it and the disciples found it true (Acts 1:5; 2:1–4). Have you received the Holy Spirit? (19:1–6). You may, for the promise is as fully yours today as at any time in the past (2:38, 39).[1]

Reread Acts 2:1–4. Who received the filling with the Holy Spirit in verse 4?

Who was left out, not receiving the promised filling with the Holy Spirit?

How many people were gathered in the Upper Room that day (1:15)?

In verse 2 what did they hear?

✎ WORD WEALTH

Spirit, *pneuma:* Compare "pneumonia," "pneumatology," "pneumatic." Breath, breeze, a current of air, wind, spirit. *Pneuma* is that part of a person capable of responding to God. The Holy Spirit is the third person of the Trinity, who draws us to Christ, convicts us of sin, enables us to accept Christ as our personal Savior, assures us of salvation, and enables us to live the victorious life, understand the Bible, pray according to God's will, and share Christ with others.[2]

Acts 2:3 describes what was seen that day. What was upon each person?

How does this experience relate to Jesus' words in:
Matthew 3:11

Luke 3:16

In Acts 2:4, what was the miracle sign that they *all* received?

Peter in Acts 10 is instructed by the Holy Spirit to preach to Gentiles in Caesarea. During his time of ministry those who were gathered to listen to Peter had a remarkable experience in Cornelius's house (10:22). In Acts 10:44 what happened to "all those who heard the word" which Peter preached?

Acts 10:45 says, "the gift of the Holy Spirit had been poured out on the Gentiles also." In 10:46, what is the reason Peter and his companions knew the Gentiles had received the Holy Spirit?

Later, in describing the miracle at Cornelius's house, Peter declares, "the Holy Spirit fell upon them," Acts 11:15. What is the phrase used in 11:16 for this same experience?

THE BAPTISM WITH THE HOLY SPIRIT IN THE BOOK OF ACTS

There are a number of phrases used in Acts for the experience of the believer having a dynamic personal encounter with the Holy Spirit, each synonymous with the baptism with the Holy Spirit. What is the word or phrase used concerning this encounter with the Holy Spirit in:

1:5	9:17
2:4	10:44
2:38	11:16
8:15	19:6
8:16	

In these nine references there are five passages where people experience Holy Spirit baptism. Each one is different, however there are some similarities you will notice as you study the events.

In Acts 2:1–4, what were the supernatural experiences of those in the Upper Room?

What did they hear in verse 2?

What did they see in verse 3?

Who was "filled" in verse 4?

What did they do as a result of being filled?

In Acts 8:14–19 the apostles Peter and John went to Samaria "that they might receive the Holy Spirit," verse 15. What happened in verse 17?

What supernatural sign accompanied the Samaritans when they received the Holy Spirit in this passage?

Why did Simon want to buy the apostles' power?

BEHIND THE SCENES

Simon the Magus or "the magician" in Acts 8 was converted to Christ after he had held Samaria under his power as a local shaman. As Philip comes on the scene the power of God is demonstrated to be much greater than Simon's ability to bewitch the people. Simon converts to Christ and is baptized in water. However, his attempt to buy Holy Spirit power is thoroughly rejected by Peter, who understands the impure motive of Simon's heart. Many believe Simon left for Cyprus and is found again in Acts 13:6–8 as he is attempting to beguile Sergius Paulus, the proconsul of the island. Later tradition places Simon as a constant adversary to Peter in his ministry. Finally, history records elsewhere that Simon plunged to his death while attempting to impress Roman leaders with his ability to fly. Tradition has it that he failed as a result of Peter's prayers.[3]

In Acts 9:17–18, Paul is "filled with the Holy Spirit." What miracle happened in verse 18?

In Acts 10:44–48 the first Gentiles came to faith in Christ and the Holy Spirit "fell upon all those who heard the word," (v. 44). Which of the Gentiles had the Holy Spirit fall upon them?

What was "poured out" on the Gentiles in verse 45?

What was the miracle evidence in verse 46?

Why did the Jews present recommend water baptism in verse 47?

In Acts 19:1–7 the Ephesians received Paul's ministry and were baptized in the name of Jesus Christ (v. 5). What did Paul do in verse 6?

What miracle sign occurred in verse 6?

How did Paul know they had received the Holy Spirit?

In these five events, three include the miracle manifestation of tongues. This is the only manifestation that occurs more than one time as a result of Holy Spirit baptism. The two events where tongues are not recorded at the time of Holy Spirit baptism have interesting circumstances concerning them. First, in Samaria (Acts 8) there was an obvious miracle sign which caused

Simon Magus to desire to purchase this power. What was the sign? We are not told. Could it have been tongues? Second, in Paul's experience with being filled with the Holy Spirit (Acts 9), tongues are not mentioned. However, read 1 Corinthians 14:18. Does Paul speak with tongues?

THE NECESSITY OF UNITY

What shall we conclude from our study of these passages? Tongues is recorded as happening on most of the occasions. The absence of the mention of tongues in Samaria and Paul's initial experience do not guarantee they were not present. However, neither can it be proved beyond doubt that they were.

Many Pentecostal and charismatic groups hold to the doctrine of tongues as the "initial evidence" of Holy Spirit baptism. There is ample reason to believe that tongues were so normal in the early church that the absence of reference to them may have simply been because Luke presumed them to be present.

On the other hand, many charismatic and non-charismatic believers reject the notion that tongues is always the initial evidence of Holy Spirit baptism. They insist that there are other miracle manifestations which may occur "initially" to demonstrate Holy Spirit baptism—such as healing in Paul's case in Acts 9, or some other miracle that may have occurred in Acts 8 at Samaria.

The tragedy is that this doctrine should be used to divide the church. Those who speak with tongues they have proof. Those who do not, they are made to feel incomplete in their Christian experience as a result. Without an airtight witness of Scripture on the subject it is best we always remain charitable with each, remembering Jesus' prayer in John 17.

Look up the following verses on the topic of unity. Write down what they say and how that could apply to the controversy of "initial evidence."

Psalm 133:1

1 Corinthians 1:10

2 Corinthians 13:11

Ephesians 4:3

Ephesians 4:13

Philippians 1:27

Colossians 2:2

1 Peter 3:8

 KINGDOM EXTRA

Being "of one accord" is a dominant trait of New Testament leadership. Whenever the early church leaders gathered in Jerusalem, it is said they were in unity and harmony, with each other and with God (2:46; 4:24; 5:12; 15:25). Their agreement was spiritual and practical, not only theological, for they shared their lives and possessions. Acts 2:42–47 gives a description of New Testament leadership: meeting together, studying together, sharing their material possessions (2:45; 4:32–37; 6:1). They met often to pray, revealing not only relationship with each other but their total reliance on God (2:42; 4:31; 12:5; 13:3).[4]

FAITH ALIVE

What has your experience with the baptism with the Holy Spirit been?

What do you think of the topic of tongues as "initial evidence"?

Has it ever been a challenge between you and other believers?

How do you think that believers can enter into unity and agreement on this topic?

1. *Spirit-Filled Life Bible* (Nashville, TN: Thomas Nelson Publishers, 1991), 1622, "Kingdom Dynamics: Acts 1:3–8, Receiving Kingdom Power."
2. Ibid., 1697, "Word Wealth: Rom. 7:6, Spirit."
3. James Orr, *International Standard Bible Encyclopedia,* (Grand Rapids, MI: William B. Eerdman Publishing Co., 1980), vol. 4, 2795–2797, "Simon Magus" by John Rutherford.
4. *Spirit-Filled Life Bible,* 1623, "Kingdom Dynamics: Acts 1:14, Unity and Harmony."

Lesson 5/The Ongoing Life of the Spirit

DISCIPLE OR BELIEVER?

One afternoon I was sitting in our family room and I decided that the finishing touch needed on one of the tables was a plant. So I went out and purchased a plant that was the perfect size, the perfect shape, and one that I couldn't kill! It looked beautiful and was indeed the finishing touch the room needed . . . for about a week and a half. In that short amount of time, it had, of course, grown and was no longer the perfect size and shape.

So I trimmed it back.

Thus began a tug of war between the plant and me: it wanted to grow and I wanted it to be the perfect size and shape. Well, the plant won! I finally moved it elsewhere and bought a silk plant to be my "finishing touch."

The bottom line in this incident was that while I believed that a plant would look beautiful in my home, I didn't want to allow any growth to take place. And that is the inherent difference between a believer and a disciple. I can *believe* in Jesus, I can trust in His salvation provision, I can accept His forgiveness, I am His *child* . . . but until growth starts to take place, I haven't become a *disciple*.

 WORD WEALTH

Disciples, *mathetes:* From the verb *manthano,* "to learn," whose root *math* suggests thought with effort put forth. A disciple is a learner, one who follows both the teaching and the teacher. The word is used first of the Twelve and later of Christians generally.[1]

Scripture describes our life in Jesus as constantly moving from level to level, growing, and progressing. Look up the following verses and write down what Scripture says our life will be like as we follow the Lord and His ways.

2 Samuel 22:37

Psalm 84:7

Psalm 92:12

Proverbs 4:18

John 10:10

2 Corinthians 3:18

Philippians 3:13–14

Hebrews 12:1

Life in the Lord is not a static, stagnant existence—"I've got my 'fire insurance' . . . I'm saved." It even goes beyond "being able to talk in tongues." Living in God's kingdom isn't a matter of personal attainment, of "showing off what I can do." Jack Hayford writes, "It is possible that nothing more thwarts Christian growth than the pretentiousness of any pattern of *posturing*, of supposed 'attainment,' however piously manifest.

"Such a 'static' state of imagined accomplishment preempts the dynamic growth the Lord intends for us. Jesus described our relationship with Him as vine-to-branch, and in doing so not only promised growth but demanded fruitfulness."[2]

Rather than just a stagnant existence, the Lord calls us to be heirs with Christ (Gal. 4:7) and to reign as kings and priests (Rev. 1:6). God has adopted us as His children and placed us now in His kingdom. There is a whole new life full of possibilities (John 10:10), adventure (Dan. 11:32), development of new abilities (Matt. 25:14–30), new growth potential (Eph. 2:21), and continual fulfillment of God's promises to us in Christ (2 Pet. 1:4).

 KINGDOM EXTRA

Colossians 1:13 describes the "transference" of the believer, from under Satan's authority to Christ's, as movement into another "kingdom." Ensuing verses describe Christ's redemption as bringing us to a place of "completeness," that is, of spiritual adequacy, authority, or ability to live victoriously over and above the invisible powers of darkness (vv. 14–16; 2:6–10). This becomes functionally true, as opposed to merely theoretically so, when we 1) live and love as citizens of the heavenly kingdom (Phil. 3:20); 2) utilize this kingdom's currency, which is of irresistible value (Acts 3:6); 3) operate as ambassadors authorized to offer kingdom peace and reconciliation to those yet unrenewed in Christ (2 Cor. 5:20); and 4) serve as the kingdom militia, girded for prayerful conflict against the dark powers controlling so much of this present world (Eph. 6:10–20). The terminology of "the kingdom" holds more than poetic pictures. It is practically applicable to all our living.[3]

As great as our initial salvation is—and it *IS* great!—the Lord offers us much more in our lives and in the growth process. To set all of that aside to "just be saved" is to deny all of the gifts the Lord has put in us. It's wishing the baby would just stay a baby, because he or she is so cute, rather than facilitating the development of that child so that he or she reaches their ultimate potential and destiny. That's what God has ahead for us!

But like the little child, all of that destiny can't be put into his or her hands at once . . . the child is not capable of handling it yet; it requires a growth process.

HOLINESS—PART OF THE GROWTH PROCESS

Personal growth requires personal discipline, and basic to that concept is the commitment to holiness of life. For many people the word "holy" immediately conjures up ideas of people who are "too good" for anyone else. The don't walk, they float. They don't talk, they pontificate. They don't eat, they "sup." And, of course, they probably don't sleep at all because they're "busy about the Father's work." At least that's our idea of "holiness." And it seems so unattainable. But Scripture teaches a different approach to holiness—our holiness grows as we grow closer to Jesus, becoming more like Him.

 KINGDOM EXTRA

If it were not possible to live a holy life, God would not have commanded it. He said, "You shall be holy, for I the Lord your God am holy" (Lev. 19:2). To be holy means to be separated to God. God's nature itself defines holiness. Being set apart to God makes us holy.

We are *not* made holy by doing good things. We *are* made holy by faith in Christ, just as we are saved by faith. Little by little, as we grow and live with the Lord, we will become more like Him (2 Cor. 3:18).

If you are a Christian, ten years from now your life should be considerably different from what it is now. Your motives and desires, as you draw closer to Him, should be continuously more holy. Although perfection is not totally attainable in this life, it is something we should constantly strive toward and aim for, for Christian maturity and holy living constitute being a responsible son or daughter of God.[4]

Look up these Scriptures that talk about purity and holiness of life. Write down what they tell us we are to do.

Psalm 24:4, 5

Proverbs 15:26

Matthew 5:8

Now look up the following verses that tell of Jesus' desire for us to grow in holiness and His promise to us to be the One who effects that growth in us.

Ephesians 1:4; 5:27; Colossians 1:21, 22; 1 Thessalonians 3:13

    KINGDOM EXTRA

The privilege of becoming an authorized and empowered representative of God's kingdom and of ministering Christ's life and the Holy Spirit's gifts to others is not the heritage of the unholy. Twice 1 Corinthians 6:9, 10 says certain people will not "inherit the kingdom of God," and then designates broad categories of people who are excluded from enjoying the resources and rewards of righteousness. (See also Gal. 5:19–21; Eph. 5:5.)

Although our righteousness before God is through Christ's work alone, and while it remains timelessly true that we cannot earn any spiritual gift or right to function in the power of the Holy Spirit, integrity and morality of character are nonetheless essential to the "kingdom person."

Holiness of heart and life keeps the lines of communication with God unjumbled, by keeping any private or carnal agenda out of the way. They also ensure the Holy Spirit free access for distributing His gifts and fulfilling the Father's will in any situation.[5]

THE DISCIPLE'S DISCIPLINES

The scriptural perspective regarding discipline is very wide in its scope. Turn to and read Hebrews 12:3–11. While outwardly this may look like punishment for wrongdoing, further study of the text and language used actually reveals a deeper purpose for discipline.

WORD WEALTH

Chasten, *paideuo:* Hebrews 12:10 tells us that God chastens us for "our profit, that we may be partakers of His holiness." On the surface it sounds like the typical "this is gonna hurt me more than it hurts you" speech. Yet the word *paideuo* itself helps us to a greater understanding. *Paideuo* literally means to train up a child, to educate, or (by implication) to discipline (by punishment). Thus we see that all of God's chastening or discipline isn't just punishment; much of it is also to instruct us and bring us to greater understanding in Him.[6]

In requiring discipline of us, God is ultimately making us "partakers of His holiness." Let's turn now to look at some of the personal disciplines that help us to grow to maturity in Christ.

PRAYER

A daily time of intimate fellowship with the Father is essential to our growth and our life in the Spirit.

KINGDOM EXTRA

In John 4:32, when Jesus refused the food offered by His disciples and declared, "I have food to eat of which you do not know," He was not implying that physical hunger and thirst were sinful (He later made eating and drinking sacramental signs). But His spirit's hunger had priority over physical appetites. He found satisfying food in deep communion with God and in doing His Father's will. Applause and material acquisitions can feed vanity and nourish ambition, but they cannot sustain the spirit. A prayerful quest for God will lead to our finding our food, our spiritual strength and satisfaction in doing God's will. And, like Jesus, we shall discover God's will through daily communion with Him; and we shall receive a fresh, daily anointing to achieve it.[7]

Look up these verses on prayer and write down how each teaches you to prioritize times of prayer in your life.

Matthew 7:7; 21:22; 26:41; Luke 18:1; John 14:13, 14; Romans 12:12; Philippians 4:6; 1 Thessalonians 5:17; 1 Timothy 2:8; James 4:2, 3; 5:15; 1 Peter 4:7; 1 John 3:22

Now look up the following verses and answer the questions on how the Holy Spirit affects our attitude toward the Father: Galatians 4:6; Romans 8:15.

What creates our *desire* to spend time in prayer?

How is the Holy Spirit operating in these two verses?

Look up these two verses that talk about prayer in the Spirit and write down what they teach us: Romans 8:26; 1 Corinthians 14:15.

Do you think these two verses are discussing prayer in spiritual language? Why or why not?

BEING WITH THE BODY

Scripture also tells us that a basic need and discipline of God's children is to be with the family. Not only does fellowship provide an environment for growth and edification, it provides us with opportunities for concerted prayer and ministry to one another. Look up Luke 4:16 and write down the phrase that describes Jesus' pattern of worship attendance.

Now, look up these verses that tell us how the early church viewed the importance of being with the body.

Luke 24:52, 53

Acts 2:1, 42, 46; 5:42

2 Corinthians 8:4; Philippians 1:3, 5

Hebrews 10:25; 1 John 1:7

Look up Galatians 3:5 and write down how the presence of the Holy Spirit is to be in effect in our gatherings together.

What is the answer to Paul's question in this verse? How might "the hearing of faith" relate to the importance of the Word in our gatherings?

BEING IN THE WORD

Scripture establishes the Word as the foundation of our faith, beliefs, and doctrines (2 Tim. 3:16); as a name given to Jesus, our Savior (John 1:1); as that which holds all of creation together (John 1:3; Hebrews 1:3); as enduring forever (Matt. 24:35; 1 Pet. 1:25); as food for our souls (1 Pet. 2:2); and as a purifier of our lives (Ps. 119:9; John 17:17).

KINGDOM EXTRA

Purity of life is not a quest for perfection as much as it is a quest for liberation from those things that may inhibit effectiveness and reduce power-filled living. This text shows the Word of God as a means of reflection—a mirror into which we are to look and see ourselves. The call is not only to heed what we see and accept the Bible's corrective instruction, but there is an unwritten lesson here. We should avoid the temptation to see (and judge) others in the Word, analyzing what they ought to do, instead of what we need to do. Second

Corinthians 3:18 also likens God's Word to a mirror, but describes the image seen as no less than the Lord Jesus Himself. The sum of the two texts: 1) The Bible shows us Christ's likeness in order that 2) we may measure our conduct and character against His and allow God to shape us into Christ's likeness (Rom. 8:29). Other promises for cleansing through God's Word: Jer. 29:9 speaks of the "fire" in the Word, which can purge as well as ignite; and Ps. 119:9 holds special promise to the one who wants a pure life of holy power. God's Word is a powerful, cleansing, delivering agent.[8]

Look up these verses that tell us to be in the Word. Write down the insights each verse gives on the importance of the Word in our lives, and how it may affect our growth.

Deuteronomy 11:19; 17:19

Job 23:12

Psalm 19:8; 119:47

Jeremiah 15:16

John 5:39

Acts 17:11

Romans 15:4

Ephesians 5:26

2 Timothy 2:15

1 Peter 1:22; 2:2

 KINGDOM EXTRA

Beginning in 1 Cor. 2:10, Paul elaborates our need of Holy Spirit-given wisdom and revelation, and he ties this very firmly to our receiving the "words . . . which the Holy Spirit teaches" (2:13). He immediately turns from these observations to an outright confrontation with the carnality of the Corinthians, attributing it to the shallowness of their intake of God's Word ("not able to receive [solid food]," 3:2; see also Heb. 5:12–15).

The demanding truth of this passage is that no amount of supposed spiritual insight or experience reflects genuine spiritual growth, if it is separated from our basic growth in the knowledge of God's Word in the Bible. Without this rootedness in the Word, we may be deluded about our growth. Such "rootedness" is in <u>truth</u> and <u>love</u>, not merely in <u>earning knowledge</u> or accomplished <u>study</u>. In order to experience true spiritual growth, we must spend time in the Word and separate ourselves from the hindrances of lovelessness, competitiveness, and strife.[9]

Look up these verses and write down how the Holy Spirit increases the effect of God's Word in our lives.

Nehemiah 9:20

Luke 12:12

John 16:13

John 14:26

1 Corinthians 2:10–13

TITHE

Look up and write out Malachi 3:10, then answer the questions below.

God never commands us to do something without purpose behind it. What do you think God's purpose is in having us learn to tithe?

Look up Matthew 23:23 to see Jesus' view on tithing. Was Jesus telling people to stop tithing? What phrase tells you that Jesus viewed tithing as a valid practice?

Look up these other verses on tithing in Scripture: Genesis 14:20; 28:22; Leviticus 27:30; 2 Chronicles 31:5

 KINGDOM EXTRA

Many people are handicapped by their own poverty, and too often their poverty is caused by their own disobedience to the Word. There are many ways in which people are disobedient; one way is in robbing God! Malachi 3:8–10 clearly tells us that those who withhold their tithes and offerings are robbing God. As a consequence, they are also robbing themselves of the blessings that God wants to bestow upon them. You see, when you do not tithe you are breaking the law; and if you are breaking the law, then the benevolent law of God cannot work on your behalf. Nothing will keep a wise believer from tithing and giving, but he or she will never be found to tithe or give offerings just to get something in return. Rather, the act arises from obedience, and God <u>always</u> rewards obedience.[10]

God wants us to learn to tithe for a twofold purpose: 1) He wants us to learn to put our trust in Him, not in material things, and 2) He wants us to learn to give—of ourselves, of our time, and of our possessions. Look up the following verses on giving and write down what they say about the requirements and results of giving in our lives.

Deuteronomy 16:17

Proverbs 3:9

Malachi 3:11: What promise does God give us as a result of our faithfulness to tithing?

Matthew 10:8

Matthew 19:21

Luke 6:38

Acts 3:6: What example does Peter set for us here?

1 Corinthians 16:2

2 Corinthians 9:7

How do you think learning to give will affect our spiritual growth?

How do you think the presence of the Holy Spirit in our lives affects our giving?

Read Psalm 51:12. What word is used to describe the Spirit of God? What implication does that have for us?

 KINGDOM EXTRA

God is not opposed to Christians having material things. He is opposed to material things "having," or controlling, Christians. Mark 10:17–27 tells us the story of the rich young ruler. The young man in this passage had kept the Law all his life, but his riches controlled him rather than his controlling the riches. He could not let go of those material things—not even for eternal life. There is no reason to doubt that if he had let those material things go, Jesus would have told him to keep them. This episode is a sad example of what can happen when people begin to trust in their material goods instead of trusting in God who has provided them.[11]

ACCEPTING MINISTRY, SERVICE, AND WITNESS

Jesus' intent for the church was never to live in some kind of exclusive, ivory tower existence. Look up these verses and write down what Jesus' intent for the church is.

Matthew 28:18–20

Mark 16:15–18

Luke 24:45–48

John 20:21–23

That is Jesus' intent for the church, and in Luke 24:49 and Acts 1:8, He promised the power to fulfill that mission. Acts 2:1–4 tells the account of the outpouring of the Holy Spirit to empower God's people for ministry. Look up these three Scriptures and write down what you think their implication is for you.

If Jesus commissioned the church, and then empowered the church for ministry, it's logical to assume that He expected the church to live in ministry—serving the world around them and bearing witness to the gospel of Christ. Look up these verses on service and witness and write down what they say we are to do.

Isaiah 43:10

Matthew 10:42; Mark 10:43, 44; Luke 10:36, 37

John 12:26; 13:14; 15:27

Acts 22:15

Galatians 5:13; 6:10

Titus 2:15

KINGDOM EXTRA

To understand the Great Commission in Mark, we must capture the spirit of Mark's focus on Jesus as the Servant. Messianic prophecies, such as Isaiah 42:1–21; 49:1–7; 50:4–11; 53:12, forecast Jesus' servant-character would do a specific work and act with unqualified and unsullied obedience.

Mark shows Christ's servant-character by omitting His genealogy (by which other Gospels establish His identity), showing that, as servants of Christ, we, too, might learn the servant-spirit essential to fulfilling the Great Commission. Christ seeks those who will serve without seeking recognition, selflessly and obediently seeking to exalt Christ and make Him known. Such servants establish their personhood and ministries by their devotion and obedience to Jesus, their disposition to serve unselfishly—their only exercise of power being to extend the love of God—ministering His life to the lost, the sick, and those in bondage. They do so wherever and however God sovereignly directs, whether it be through their giving, their going, or their prayerful intercession. The Servant Jesus' love and obedience compel His servants to loyal and unreserved service.[12]

FAITH ALIVE

We've reviewed some very powerful discipleship patterns. Now it's time to make some honest analysis, with the help of the Holy Spirit, to determine where the strong and weak points are in your spiritual growth process.

1. Prayer
   Do you spend time each day in prayer?
   Is it a specific time of day?
   Do you have a prayer list to help guide you?
   Is the Lord calling you to a higher commitment in this area?
2. Being with the Body
   Are you a member of a local congregation?
   Do you attend church services regularly?

Do you spend fellowship time with other believers?

Do you need to increase the amount of time you spend with other believers?

3. Being in the Word

Do you read your Bible every day?

Do you follow a Bible reading plan or skip around in your reading?

Have you read through the entire Bible?

Do you have a Scripture memorization plan?

4. Tithe

Do you tithe to your local congregation?

Do you give in additional ways—offerings, time, talents?

Are there areas of your financial life that you have not brought into submission to the Lord?

Is the Lord challenging you to give more in any of these ways, or with a different attitude?

5. Accepting Ministry, Service, and Witness

Are you involved in an area of ongoing service or ministry?

Are you involved in areas that touch both believers and unbelievers?

Are you equipped to share your faith with an unbeliever?

Ask the Lord to give you the names of five unbelievers to carry in prayer that they will be saved.

1. *Spirit-Filled Life Bible* (Nashville, TN: Thomas Nelson Publishers, 1991), 1421, "Word Wealth: Matt. 10:1, disciples."

2. Jack Hayford, *The Beauty of Spiritual Language* (Dallas, TX: Word Publishers, 1992), page 58.

3. *Spirit-Filled Life Bible*, 1813, "Kingdom Dynamics: Col. 1:13, People of the Kingdom."

4. Ibid., 1998, "Spiritual Answers to Hard Questions: Can I live a holy life? (Matt. 5:8)."

5. Ibid., 1726, "Kingdom Dynamics: 1 Cor. 6:9, 10, Integrity and Morality."

6. James Strong, *New Strong's Exhaustive Concordance* (Nashville, TN: Thomas Nelson Publishers, 1984), "Dictionary of the Greek Testament" #3811.

7. *Spirit-Filled Life Bible*, 1580; "Kingdom Dynamics: John 4:34, A Prayerful Quest for God Is the Pathway to Satisfaction."

8. Ibid., 1896, "Kingdom Dynamics: James 1:23–25, God's Word: Purifier unto Holy Living."

9. Ibid., 1722, "Kingdom Dynamics: 1 Cor. 3:1–5, True Spiritual Growth Requires God's Word."

10. Ibid., 1387, "Kingdom Dynamics: Mal. 3:8–10, God's Prosperity Plan Includes Tithing."

11. Ibid., 1490, "Kingdom Dynamics: Mark 10:17–27, Using Things, Not Loving Them."

12. Ibid., 1502, "Kingdom Dynamics: Mark 16:15–18, Commissioned in Christ's Servant Spirit."

Lesson 6/The Song of the Spirit

Picture this: A cozy mountain cabin. A fire flickers on the hearth. The dining table is set, and candles fill the room with a soft glow. The harmonic chords of a symphony permeate the atmosphere, setting a serene mood for an evening of rest and relaxation.

Now picture this: A teenager's bedroom. The walls are painted black, and there are posters of rock and roll musicians all over the room. The air fairly reeks with the strident beat and discord of heavy metal music.

Last picture: A church service. The congregation is being led in worship. Beautiful accompaniment is coming from the hands of the instrumentalists. Eyes are closed and hands are raised as each person lifts his or her voice in praise. Time is not a concern right now. It is an intimate moment before the throne of God.

SONG AND PRAISE ARE LINKED

No matter what the situation, music has a way of instantly establishing both *attitude* and *atmosphere*—for good or bad. For this reason, music has always been a primary part of the worship of God's people, and spiritual song provides us with a tool for not only establishing an atmosphere of praise, but for inviting the very presence of God's kingdom rule as well.

The first incident we see in Scripture of a song of praise is in Exodus 15. The Lord has just brought Israel through the Red Sea, and now the entire congregation lifts their voices in praise to their deliverer. But this is just the first of many! Scripture tells us of the morning stars singing at creation (Job 38:7); singers were appointed over the temple worship (1 Chr. 9:33); we are told that the Lord sings over us (Zeph. 3:17); and throughout eternity, we will sing a new song to the Lord (Rev. 5:9 and 14:3).

Look up the following Scriptures that show the use of song in praise. Write down the different ways and the varying situations in which praise in song is employed.

Judges 4:23–5:1

Deuteronomy 31:19, 22

2 Chronicles 20:1–4, 14–22

 KINGDOM EXTRA

Second Chronicles 20 provides us with a great lesson on the power of praise. Judah was confronted by mortal enemies, Moab and Ammon. The people sought God in prayer and with faith in His Word (20:1–14). Then came the word of the prophet: "Do not be afraid . . . for the battle *is* not yours, but God's" (v. 15).

The victory came in a strange but powerful manner. The Levites stood and praised "the Lord God of Israel with voices *loud and high*" (v. 19). Then some were actually appointed to sing to the Lord and praise Him in the beauty of holiness. These went before the army, saying: "Praise the Lord, for His mercy *endures* [lasts] forever" (v. 21). The result of this powerful praise was total victory![1]

Ezra 3:11

Isaiah 24:14; 26:19; 49:13; 52:9; 54:1

Mark 14:26

Acts 16:25–34

KINGDOM EXTRA

Study Acts 16 to see this example of the power of praise, even in difficult circumstances. Beaten and imprisoned, Paul and Silas respond by singing a hymn of praise—a song sung directly from the heart to God. The relationship between their song of praise and their supernatural deliverance through the earthquake cannot be overlooked. Praise directed toward God can shake open prison doors! A man was converted, his household saved, and satanic captivity overthrown in Philippi. Today, as well, praise will cause every chain of bondage to drop away. When you are serving God and things do not go the way you planned, learn from this text. Praise triumphs gloriously![2]

Romans 15:9

Hebrews 2:12

Look up these verses that command us to sing: Exodus 15:21; Numbers 21:16, 17; Psalm 47:6; 81:1; 100:2; Isaiah 42:10; Zephaniah 3:14; Zechariah 2:10; James 5:13

KINGDOM EXTRA

Much of what we learn about praise in the Old Testament is taken directly from the Psalms—Israel's hymnal. The Psalms conclude with a mighty appeal to praise the Lord (Ps. 150:1–6). Some psalms are desperate cries, some filled with thanksgiving, and some have theologically or historically based instructions to "praise the Lord" for His own Person, holiness, power, or goodness. But the climax is a command to praise the Lord. We are to praise God 1) <u>in His sanctuary</u>—that is, His earthly temple and throughout His created universe and 2) <u>for His mighty acts</u> and according to <u>His excellent greatness</u>. Then a list of instruments and ways to praise follows. This list is not exhaustive but demonstrates how creative our praise is to be. Finally, in case even one person feels less than inclined to praise Him, the instruction is clear: If you have God's gift of life-breath, you should praise Him. Hallelujah![3]

Scripture also talks about praise being a choice we make, and in some cases, even a sacrifice that we present before the Lord. Look up these verses and write down what each says about how our will is involved in praising the Lord.

Judges 5:3

2 Samuel 22:50

Psalm 9:2; 27:6; 59:17

Isaiah 61:3

Hebrews 13:15

 KINGDOM EXTRA

Why is praising God a sacrifice? The word "sacrifice" (Greek *thusia*) comes from the root *thuo,* a verb meaning "to kill or slaughter for a purpose." Praise often requires that we "kill" our pride, fear, or sloth—anything that threatens to diminish or interfere with our worship of the Lord. We also discover here the basis of all our praise: the sacrifice of our Lord Jesus Christ. It is by Him, in Him, with Him, to Him, and for Him that we offer our sacrifice of praise to God. Praise will never be successfully hindered when we keep its focus on Him—the Founder and Completer of our salvation. His Cross, His Blood—His love gift of life and forgiveness to us—keep praise as a living sacrifice![4]

THE SWEET PSALMIST OF ISRAEL

As we've seen, praise in song is woven throughout the entire Word. However, it is probably most clearly seen in the life of David. Look up these verses and write down the times in David's life when song in praise was used.

1 Samuel 16:14–23; 18:6, 7

2 Samuel 1:17–27; 3:33

2 Samuel 6:12–15, 20, 21; 22:1

1 Chronicles 13:8; 15:26–28; 16:7

1 Chronicles 23:1–2, 30; 25:1; 29:9–10

Other times of David praising in song are accounted in the Psalms. Look up these and write down other circumstances in which David praised God. (Be sure to read the subheadings of each Psalm.)

Psalm 3 (See 2 Sam. 15:1–17.)

Psalm 18 (See 2 Sam. 22.)

 KINGDOM EXTRA

Here is the most basic reason for our praise to God; He is "*worthy* to be praised [Hebrew *halal,* 'praise with a loud voice']." The most primitive meaning of *halal* is "to cause to shine." Thus, with our praise, we are throwing the spotlight on our God who is worthy and deserves to be praised and glorified.

The more we put the spotlight on Him, the more He causes us to shine. Modern medicine attests to the value of bringing depressed persons into a brightly lighted room, acknowledging that light greatly helps to heal their depression. How much more will praise introduce the light of God and bring us into the joy of the Lord.[5]

Psalm 30 (See 1 Chr. 14:1.)

Psalm 51 (See 2 Sam. 11:1—12:15.)

Psalm 54 (See 1 Sam. 23:19.)

Psalm 57 (See 1 Sam. 24:3.)

Psalm 60 (See 2 Sam. 8:13.)

Psalm 142 (See 1 Sam. 22:1.)

 ### FAITH ALIVE

Go back over the list of incidents where David praised the Lord in song. Can you think of similar examples in your own life where song in praise would be effective? (For example, you may not face a literal giant like Goliath, but there may be a situation that seems like something "bigger than you.") Write these down and then spend some time with the Lord in song, praise, and worship.

INVITING GOD'S RULE

David learned something that most of us have not: praise and worship establish an *atmosphere* that invites God's rulership to be where we are!

KINGDOM EXTRA

The Psalms were the praise hymnal of the early church, and as such are laden with principles fully applicable for New Testament living today. Few principles are more essential to our understanding than this one: the <u>presence</u> of God's kingdom power is directly related to the practice of God's praise. The verb "enthroned" indicates that wherever God's people exalt His name, He is ready to manifest His kingdom's power in the way most appropriate to the situation, as His rule is invited to invade our setting.

It is this fact that properly leads many to conclude that in a very real way, praise prepares a <u>specific</u> and <u>present</u> place for God among His people. Some have chosen the term "establish His throne" to describe this "enthroning" of God in our midst by our worshipping and praising welcome. God awaits the prayerful and praise-filled worship of His people as an entry point for His kingdom to "come"—to enter, that <u>His</u> "will be done" in human circumstances. (See Luke 11:2–4 and Ps. 93:2.) We do not manipulate God, but align ourselves with the great kingdom truth: <u>His</u> is the power, ours is the privilege (and responsibility) to welcome Him into our world—our private, present world or the circumstances of our society."[6]

Let's look closer at the episode of the ark of the covenant being brought to Jerusalem in 2 Samuel 6 and the Lord's subsequent covenant with David in chapter 7 to see how God's throne was established in David's kingdom. Begin by reading these two chapters and then answer the questions below.

What does David desire to do (6:1, 2)?

Why is the presence of the ark significant? (See Ex. 25:22.)

How was the ark to be moved, according to the Mosaic Law? (See Ex. 25:14, 15; Num. 4:15–20; 7:9.)

Why do you think God made these rules? What do you think He was trying to communicate about how His people come into His presence?

Compare 6:3–8 and 6:12–18. What is the difference in attitude, action, and obedience between these two attempts to move the ark?

What did David learn from the first attempt?

How do you think the second attempt reflects the kingship of the Lord coming into the midst of His people? What lessons might this have for us today?

Verses 6:20–23 seem to be a digression from the main theme of the chapter, but let's look at them in terms of Michal's attitude toward the arrival of the ark. What did her attitude appear to be? What was the ultimate result in her life of not appropriately valuing the presence of God? What lessons can we draw from Michal's life?

What did David desire to do in 7:2?

What is God's response (7:5–7)? Was He angry? How do we know?

What is God's promise to David (7:11–16)?

What does 7:18 tell us about David's desire to be in the Lord's presence? What does it say about his assurance of acceptance? How do you think the incident with Uzzah may have affected David's attitude in God's presence?

What was David's attitude toward the promise God had given him (7:26, 27)? What was his attitude toward the Lord (7:28)?

What do you think is the correlation of God establishing David's kingdom forever and David's desire to invite God's presence to be where he was?

 KINGDOM EXTRA

"Your throne is established from of old." The notion that kingdom advance "establishes" God's throne needs clearer understanding. It is foolish to think man could add to or diminish the power or glory of God's kingdom rule. However, it is equally unwise to overlook the responsible place the redeemed have been given. We are to welcome the kingdom and administrate situations on Earth by inviting the overarching might of God's Spirit to move into difficult or impossible circumstances and transform them. This is done by praise: "In everything [not "for" everything] give thanks [fill the situation with praise], for this is God's will for you" (1 Thess. 5:17). Thus we welcome the overruling power of God's presence into any situation we face. Pray, "Your kingdom come, Your will be done—here." Then, set up a place for God's throne to enter by filling your life's settings with praise. As Gideon's trumpeters (Judg. 7:17–22) and Jehoshaphat's choir (2 Chr. 20:20–22) confounded their enemies and paved the way for the victory the Lord said He would give, so praise brings the same entry of the King's kingdom today."[7]

SINGING SPIRITUAL SONGS

We've talked about the importance of song and the principle of God's throne being established in our midst through praise. Now let's look at Holy Spirit-enabled song and how that expands our ability to worship.

The idea of singing in the Spirit is mentioned only three times in the New Testament. Look up the following verses and write down what we learn on this subject.

1 Corinthians 14:14, 15

Ephesians 5:18, 19

Colossians 3:16

✏️ WORD WEALTH

"*Hodais pneumatikais,*" the exact words in both Ephesians 5 and Colossians 3, is usually translated "spiritual songs." The first word is simply "*ode,*" the Greek term for any words which were sung. But the second word—*pneumatikais*— seems to be the key to the full meaning of this phrase.

Noting the use of *pneumatikais* elsewhere in the New Testament, the word seems to indicate Holy Spirit-filled people of character and charisma (see 1 Cor. 12:1 and Gal 6:1). Their *charism* (in the sense of their functioning in the *charisms*—gifts of the Holy Spirit) is indicated in their apparent acceptance and response to spiritual things; that is, manifestations of the Holy Spirit's gifts (1 Cor. 12:7).

This alone would not finalize a definition, except for the fact that in this same context Paul discusses "singing with the spirit and with the understanding." His distinguishing singing "with the spirit" from "singing with the understanding" points to what spiritual songs may have meant in the first-century church: an exercise separate from, yet complementary to, the singing of psalms and hymns.[8]

What do you think about the practice of singing songs in your spiritual language?

Do you think the fact that this is mentioned so infrequently should affect our acceptance of this practice (2 Tim. 3:16)?

How do you think singing in the Spirit might help you pray (Rom. 8:26; 1 Thess. 5:17)? How might it help you praise God? How might it prepare you to minister to others?

 KINGDOM EXTRA

Hebrews 2:11, 12 quotes the messianic prophecy in Psalm 22:22, showing how the Spirit of the Christ fills the New Testament church, and how Christ identifies Himself so closely with His people when they sing praises. As they do, two important things happen: 1) He joins in the song Himself, and 2) this praise releases the spirit of prophecy. The latter is in the words "I will declare Your name to My brethren." As we joyfully sing praise to our God, Christ comes to flood our minds with the glory of the Father's character ("name"). There is no doubt about it—the praises of the people in the church service release the spirit of prophetic revelation—the magnifying of God through Jesus Christ. Thus, praise introduces edification, exhortation, and comfort to bless the whole body.[9]

Spiritual song releases praise among believers and brings joy to our hearts. While the following verses do not deal *directly* with spiritual song, they *do* deal with the joy and gladness the Lord pours out into our hearts through praise in song. Look up these Scriptures and write down how spiritual language would enhance and expand our times of praise.

Job 8:21

Psalm 126:2

Proverbs 17:22

Isaiah 35:10

 ## FAITH ALIVE

Is spiritual song a part of your devotional time? How much time are you spending in praise and worship each day?

Write down the area(s) of your life that you feel would be most strengthened by spiritual song.

Get on your knees right now—Yes, right now!—and present this area of your life to the Lord. Then spend some time in the Lord's presence, as David "sat before the Lord," worshipping and singing before Him.

1. *Spirit-Filled Life Bible* (Nashville, TN: Thomas Nelson Publishers, 1991), 633, "Kingdom Dynamics: 2 Chr. 20:15–22, Powerful Praise Births Victory."

2. Ibid., 1659, "Kingdom Dynamics: Acts 16:25, 26, Praise Springs Open Prison Doors."

3. Ibid., 879, "Kingdom Dynamics: Ps. 150:1–6, A Mighty Appeal to Praise."

4. Ibid., 1890, "Kingdom Dynamics: Heb. 13:10–15, "The Sacrifice of Praise."

5. Ibid., 765, "Kingdom Dynamics: Ps. 18:3, Praise Spotlights God."

6. Ibid., 770, "Kingdom Dynamics: Ps. 22:3, "Establishing God's Throne."

7. Ibid., 835, "Kingdom Dynamics: Ps. 93:2, Inviting God's Rule."

8. Jack Hayford, *The Beauty of Spiritual Language* (Dallas, TX: Word Publishing, 1992), 193–195.

9. *Spirit-Filled Life Bible,* 1874, "Kingdom Dynamics: Heb. 2:11, 12, Praise Releases the Spirit of Prophecy."

Lesson 7/The Revelation of Truth

"I was ministering at a conference in the picturesque Ozark Mountains. One morning following the worship service a camper asked if I would be willing to talk with him about a continuing heaviness and fear that shadowed his soul.

"The first few minutes of our conversation were enough to make two things very clear: (1) he was sensible and sensitive to the Holy Spirit, and (2) there was indeed something which seemed to hinder his sense of peace and confidence as a believer, some logjam of the soul was the picture the Holy Spirit was giving me. Seeing this prophetic picture, I said, 'Have you ever seen pictures of a giant logjam on a river? A tangle snarls the forward flow of the logs.' He knew what I was depicting.

"The Holy Spirit was impressing on my heart that there was something from his past which he didn't consciously remember but was tied like a knot in his soul. After a few words of instruction I told him that I would pray briefly with him and then I would leave for ten minutes or so. 'While I'm gone,' I told him, 'I simply want you to be at prayer, for the most part, employing your spiritual language; allowing the presence of God to flow through your inner being.'

"So we joined hands and I prayed: 'Father God, we come into Your presence through the Blood of Jesus Your Son, thanking You for the fact that all our sin has been covered at His Cross. And we invite the Holy Spirit to come into this room in a special way. Only You know the deep hindering or wounding things of my brother's past. I ask You that as he worships and prays, You will bring to light any hidden, forgotten incidents which need to be dealt with.' I left as he continued praying.

"Some minutes later, I knocked at the door. He answered, inviting me in, and I opened the door to see a tear-washed face which had a look of genuine confidence. I could see by his countenance that something had happened. 'I can hardly believe it,' he began. 'The Lord has brought back to my mind two events—one when I was about five years old and the other when I was about twelve.'

"Before he began to speak them, we prayed together again. 'Lord Jesus Christ,' I prayed, 'We stand in the light before Your Throne. You are our King and our God, and it is through Your Name and Your Blood that all authority has been given to You . . . and we are in awe that You have passed that authority over sin and darkness to us. Now, as my brother speaks each of the hurtful, sinful, and injurious things in the past, we agree that *as he speaks them* these experiences will be completely loosed from his mind, his emotions, and his life! In Jesus' name. Amen.'

"'Go ahead,' I prompted him, and he began to recite the incidents in the presence of Jesus Himself, peace flooding his countenance. Several years later, I saw this brother again, still living in the freedom that had come to him that day."[1]

HE WILL GUIDE YOU INTO ALL TRUTH

In other lessons, we've talked about spiritual warfare, spiritual song, and personal discipline and how spiritual language affects those aspects of our lives. But here we will be looking at the basic ministry of the Holy Spirit in the life of the believer: He guides us into truth—truth in the Word of God and truth about ourselves.

In the Gospel of John, during the Last Supper, Jesus outlined what the coming of the Holy Spirit would mean for believers. Turn to John, look up the following references, and write down what Jesus said the Holy Spirit would do in our lives.

14:16,17

14:26

15:26

16:8, 13, 14

What appears to be the primary purpose of the ministry of the Holy Spirit?

What is the name given to the Holy Spirit in verses 14:17 and 15:26?

Look up these verses that talk about how the Holy Spirit reveals truth to us. Write down what each verse tells us.

Psalm 44:21; 139:1, 23

Jeremiah 17:10

Daniel 2:20–22

Amos 3:7

John 5:39

1 Corinthians 2:10

Ephesians 1:17; 3:3–5

Philippians 3:15

Earlier we noted that the Holy Spirit guides us into the truth of the Word and reveals truth to us about ourselves. Let's look closer at each of these aspects of the Holy Spirit at work in our lives.

THE TRUTH OF THE WORD

The Bible has been given to us as a manual for life! The Bible is the one *final* authority, closed and complete, in the sense of *biblical* revelation. But personal understanding *does* continally open and enlarge to grasp more of God's intent while *never* adding to the Bible (Eph. 1:17, 18). It is the work of the Holy Spirit that causes a fresh infusion of the truth into our lives as we meditate on the Word, and applies it to *our* circumstance through the spirit of prophecy.

BEHIND THE SCENES

"I can hardly number the times I have wrestled with a text of God's Word, seeking to gain insight into the Bible's holy truth in a way that will release its transforming power to the congregation I'll be addressing. Time and again, as I pray over Scriptures in my spiritual language—praying by the same Spirit who gave the Word initially—I've experienced the simplest-yet-most-wonderful things. It's as though the light inherent in God's Word suddenly becomes freshly alive; as though a shaft of glory from His own lips has breathed into me the same way that same Breath first breathed the words on His sacred pages. The Word will almost explode into refreshing insight at times, and on other occasions gradually open like a doorway spilling splendor into an unlighted room."[2]

Look up these verses about the inspiration of Scripture. Write down how you see the Holy Spirit at work in this process.

Jeremiah 36:2

Ezekiel 1:3

Acts 1:16

2 Timothy 3:16

2 Peter 1:21

Revelation 14:13

Now look up these verses on different ways the Word is described throughout Scripture. How do you see the Holy Spirit at work here?

Jeremiah 5:14; 23:29; Ezekiel 37:7; Ephesians 6:17; Hebrews 4:12

The following verses admonish us to be continually in the Word. In view of what we've looked at so far, why do you think being in the Word is important?

Deuteronomy 17:19; Isaiah 34:16; John 5:39; 20:31; Acts 17:11; Romans 15:4; 1 Corinthians 10:11; Ephesians 5:26

  KINGDOM EXTRA

The Bible—God's inspired Word—is the only conclusive source of wisdom, knowledge, and understanding concerning ultimate realities. It is a fountainhead of freeing truth (John 8:32) and a gold mine of practical principles (Ps. 19:10), waiting to liberate and/or enrich the person who will pursue its truth and wealth. Thus, Paul's instruction to "be diligent . . . a worker" has been applied by serious Christians through the centuries as a directive to study the Word of God. The only way to healthy, balanced living is through the "rightly dividing"

(Greek *orthotomounta,* literally, "cutting straight") of God's Word. Such correct, straight-on application of God's Word is the result of diligent study. The text calls us beyond casual approaches to the Scriptures, telling us to refuse to suit the Bible to our own convenience or ideology.

In his earlier words (1 Tim. 4:13) Paul also told Timothy, "Give attention to reading [God's Word]," but now he emphasizes <u>studying</u> like a "worker" (from Greek *ergon*—"toil, effort"). Ps. 119:11 urges memorizing of the Word of God as a mighty deterrent against sin. Memorizing the Scripture also provides an immediate availability of God's "words" as a sword, ready in witnessing and effective in spiritual warfare (Heb. 4:12; Eph. 6:17).[3]

THE TRUTH ABOUT OURSELVES

When Jesus walked the earth, He was—and still is—committed to the salvation of individuals. What we often overlook is that salvation is meant to extend to every part of our being: spirit, soul, and body.

WORD WEALTH

Salvation, *soterion:* Rescue, deliverance, safety, liberation, release, preservation, and the general word for Christian salvation. *Soterion* only occurs five times. *Soteria,* the generic word, occurs forty-five times. It is an all-inclusive word signifying forgiveness, healing, prosperity, deliverance, safety, rescue, liberation, and restoration. Christ's salvation is total in scope for the total person: spirit, soul, and body.[4]

KINGDOM EXTRA

The Greek word *sozo* ("heal, save, make well or whole") appears in Luke 8, offering Luke's unique perspective as a physician. A full range of encounters appears, manifesting Jesus' healing power: 1) The Gadarene, delivered from the demonic powers dominating him, is "healed," freed of evil powers that countermanded his own rational mind and physical actions. 2) The woman with the issue of blood (vv. 43–48) touches the hem of Jesus' garment, and Jesus says, "Your faith has made you well." 3) In v. 50, after being told the little girl is dead, Jesus declares: "Only believe, and she will be made well." 4) In v. 12, as Jesus explains the parable of the sower, the word "saved" is used of one's restored relationship with God through faith. Luke's precise account offers a complete picture of the Savior's concern to restore every part of man's life: (a) our relationship with God the Father; (b) our broken personalities and bondages; (c) our physical health; and (d) ultimately our rescue from death itself at the Resurrection. Jesus Christ is the Savior of the whole man.[5]

Probably the most challenging area of this restoration is in our souls. Spiritually and physically, things seem very straightforward: spiritually, you've either asked Jesus into your life or not; physically, you're either sick or not. But the soul is often an untapped area of our lives where emotions and thoughts can conceal or camouflage themselves—sometimes even seem to disappear altogether. Emotions can deceive, thoughts can run rampant, hardening our hearts to the Lord and those around us. Look up these verses that discuss the traits of our hearts and write down why it is so crucial for Jesus' saving restoration to penetrate to that part of our lives.

Proverbs 4:23; 23:7; Jeremiah 17:9; Matthew 5:28; 6:21

What does this tell us about what we should be treasuring?

Matthew 12:34; Mark 7:20–22; 16:14; Luke 6:45

These Scriptures present a fairly grim picture of what our souls are like without the restoration of the Holy Spirit at work in us. Look up the following verses to find out what the Lord promises He will do in our souls.

Psalm 23:3; Proverbs 10:3; Isaiah 57:17, 18; Jeremiah 30:17;
2 Corinthians 4:16

Speaking Mysteries

So how does this "revelation of truth" take place? Often it takes place through the use of our spiritual language. Does that mean that using our spiritual language is a formula we can use in situations where we want to see freedom come to our souls, our psyches? No, of course not. If there were "formulas," God would have a verse in Scripture that said, "Here is the formula for. . . ."

Yet the Lord *does* give us tools. And in this case the use of our spiritual language is a very prominent tool because "a person who prays with the Spirit is often directing that prayer toward impossible situations—convinced that 'all things are possible to him who believes' (Mark 9:23). It is the conviction that the Holy Spirit is enabling intercession—that is, prayer that will address the prayer target more efficiently—that prompts such readiness to face the impossible in faith."[6]

The apostle Paul also tells us that when we speak in our spiritual language the Holy Spirit is speaking mysteries through us (1 Cor. 14:2). In other words, through our spiritual language, the Holy Spirit can bring to light and solve "mysteries"—things in our subconscious can be brought to the forefront and solved. Bringing these issues to the "Great Psychiatrist" (for the Holy Spirit has a healing ministry different than the Great Physician's) can solve a problem, remove an obstacle, unravel a mystery in our souls that would take a professional counselor months or years to deal with . . . because it is only God who truly knows our hearts.

Look up these verses to see what Scripture says about "mysteries."

1 Corinthians 14:2; Ephesians 1:9; 3:3; Colossians 2:2

WORD WEALTH

Greek, *musterion.* From *mueo,* "to initiate into the mysteries," hence a secret known only to the initiated, something hidden requiring special revelation. In the New Testament the word denotes something that people could never know by their own understanding and that demands a revelation from God. The secret thoughts, plans, and dispensations of God remain hidden from unregenerate mankind, but are revealed to all believers. In nonbiblical Greek *musterion* is knowledge withheld, concealed, or silenced. In biblical Greek it is truth revealed (see Col. 1:26). New Testament *musterion* focuses on Christ's sinless life, atoning death, powerful resurrection, and dynamic ascension.[7]

Read these additional verses on restoration and answer the questions: Job 42:10; Isaiah 58:12–14; John 10:10.

What is God's objective for our lives through the restoration process?

Is this objective only spiritual or does it also apply to our souls and bodies?

Acts 3:19–21: What do you think repentance has to do with restoration?

What significance does the phrase "the restoration of all things" have for you?

Revelation 19:7–9: Who is "His wife"?

What significance is there for us in the phrase "His wife has made herself ready"?

What kind of restoration process has taken place in the Bride for her to be arrayed as she is in verse 8?

What personal implications does that have for the believer?

   KINGDOM EXTRA

God's work of restoration is a work of the Holy Spirit in and through the lives of those who have believed in Jesus and have been born from above (John 33). The prophet Joel foretold a day when God would pour out His Spirit "On all flesh" (Joel 2:28, 29). Thus, His power would be shared with all His people and not limited to one chosen individual. This explains why Christ told His disciples it was to their advantage for Him to leave them and go to the Father (John 16:7), because then the Spirit could be sent to indwell each of them, to fill them and to enable the supernatural works of God to be done through them.[8]

   FAITH ALIVE

How often do you use your spiritual language during times of prayer and Bible reading?

Do you keep a journal of the things the Lord teaches you and reveals to you about your life when you read the Word? How has this journal benefited your spiritual journey?

Is there a "logjam" of spirit in your life? Can you identify the source of the problem or do you need some insight from the Holy Spirit?

What is the Lord telling you to do about this situation? Has He shown you a Scripture application to make or do you think the use of your spiritual language may be a necessary tool in this circumstance?

1. Jack Hayford, *The Beauty of Spiritual Language* (Dallas, TX: Word Publishing, 1992), 143–146.

2. Ibid., 147.

3. *Spirit-Filled Life Bible* (Nashville, TN: Thomas Nelson Publishers, 1991), 1854, "Kingdom Dynamics: 2 Tim. 2:15, God's Word: Read It! Study It! Memorize It!"

4. Ibid., 1682, "Word Wealth: Acts 28:28, salvation."

5. Ibid., 1527–1528, "Kingdom Dynamics: Luke 8:36, The Healing of Spirit, Soul, and Body."

6. *The Beauty of Spiritual Language,* 68.

7. Ibid., 141.

8. *Spirit-Filled Life Bible,* 2016, "Kingdom Dynamics: Joel 2:28, 29, The Holy Spirit: The Agent of Restoration."

Lesson 8/The Public Exercise of Spiritual Language

My husband came to know the Lord when he was seventeen years old, and just a few weeks following his conversion he attended his first service in a Pentecostal church. Nothing in his traditional church background had prepared him for this gathering!

To begin with, the church service took place in a little log building in the woods considerably off the main road. He went at night . . . and being in the forest made it seem almost clandestine. But the real surprise was the service itself. A man came up to Scott and announced that he had a gift of healing for him. (Scott didn't even know he was sick!) Then a woman gave a message in tongues in nothing short of a machine-gun-like cadence. All in all, he left the service determined to have nothing more to do with Pentecostals, tongues, or the little church in the woods. (Obviously he eventually got over those feelings since he would end up becoming a Pentecostal pastor! Yes— God *does* have a sense of humor!)

However, it is situations like Scott experienced that add fuel to the debate of the use of spiritual language in public worship. Some assume, incorrectly, that the abuses should signal a need to stop the use of all spiritual language and gifts in public worship services. Yet in 1 Corinthians, we see that that was not Paul's attitude at all. The believers in Corinth had been converted out of a pagan society and in their zeal for God and their imperception of His ways, abuses had occurred. At least this congregation of baby Christians was wise enough to recognize that they needed to seek counsel and teaching. And so they had written to Paul with questions on how to grow in and live a godly life. A thorough study of 1 Corinthians will show ten areas of inquiry that Paul deals with, and in chapters 12—14, he answers the problem of spiritual manifestations which arose from a misuse of the gifts of tongues.

BEHIND THE SCENES

First Corinthians is a pastoral letter, written to resolve doctrinal and practical problems within the local church. The letter reveals some of the typical Greek cultural problems of Paul's day. The Greeks were known for their idolatry, divisive philosophies, spirit of litigation, and rejection of a bodily resurrection. It also reveals some of the problems the former pagans had in not transferring previous religious experiences to the ministry experience of the Holy Spirit. They may have associated some of the frenzied antics of paganism with the exercise of spiritual gifts (see 12:2).

No epistle in the New Testament gives a clearer insight into the life of the first-century church than 1 Corinthians. In it Paul provides straightforward instructions for such moral and theological problems as sectarianism, spiritual immaturity, church discipline, ethical differences, the role of the sexes, and the proper use of spiritual gifts. Where these same problems exist in the modern church, the remedies are the same. Those from non-pentecostal or non-charismatic churches may receive a fresh challenge from the vitality and spiritual gifts evident in the Corinthian church, and may lay aside traditional prejudices against such things. Those from charismatic and pentecostal churches, where worship is less structured and spiritual gifts are prominent, may reexamine their own practices in the light of Paul's guidelines for congregational services.[1]

THE GIFTS OF THE SPIRIT

In dealing with the public exercise of spiritual language, Paul makes clear that it isn't to be abolished, but exercised in the spirit of peace that the Holy Spirit brings. He begins in chapter 12 by discussing the diversity of the gifts of the Holy Spirit and how each gift answers a need within the body of Christ. Look up the following verses and answer the questions.

In 12:1, what is Paul's desire for the Corinthians?

Does this sound like he wants them to do away with the use of spiritual gifts?

Verses 4–6 are making the point that there is still to be unity in our diversity. How is that to be manifest?

List the gifts that Paul speaks of (vv. 8–10).

What is the point Paul is making in verse 11?

How might this verse refute the erroneous idea that some gifts are "better" than others?

Who is the author and dispenser of the gifts (vv. 1–11)?

In your own words, explain the parallel Paul draws in verses 12–27 between the differing gifts of Christ's body and the differing members and capabilities of our bodies.

How does verse 28 compare to verses 22–24?

How do verses 29, 30 compare to verse 17?

In verse 11, Paul leads us to believe that no gift is "better" than another, that every gift has its place. How does verse 31 fit into that concept?

KINGDOM EXTRA

Paul's exhortation concerning **the best gifts** seeks to correct the mistaken applications of the public use of tongues. The private use, which is designed mostly for self-edification, was being confused by public exercise. "Best" might be defined as that gift or those gifts most suited to the given situation, and an example is present: for example, prophecy is functionally "better" than tongues in public because it edifies the church (14:4, 5), unless, of course, the "tongue" is interpreted. However, the example from the human body precludes all value ranking of gifts (12:22–25). No negative conclusion about the worth of tongues may legitimately be drawn from the fact that it appears last in the lists. Is self-control the least important virtue in the fruit of the Spirit because it is listed last (Gal. 5:22, 23)? Using the same logic, love should be of less importance than faith and hope, but Paul calls it the greatest (1 Cor. 13:13).[2]

WORD WEALTH

Gift, *charisma:* Related to other words derived from the root *char. Chara* is joy, cheerfulness, delight. *Charis* is grace, goodwill, undeserved favor. *Charisma* is a gift of grace, a free gift, divine gratuity, spiritual endowment, miraculous faculty. It is especially used to designate the gifts of the Spirit (1 Cor. 12:4–10). In modern usage, a "charismatic" signifies one who either has one or more of these gifts functioning in his or her life, or who believes these gifts are for today's church.[3]

THE PRIORITY OF LOVE IN MINISTRY

Paul concludes chapter 12 with the phrase "And yet I show you a more excellent way." This phrase is also the introduction to chapter 13. Based on the preceding Kingdom Extra, write down what you think Paul is saying here.

KINGDOM EXTRA

A more excellent way is not a negative comparison between gifts and love, since the temporal adverb **yet** indicates the continuation of the subject. All manifestations of the Spirit must at the same time manifest the ways of love, for love is the ultimate issue behind all things.[4]

Chapter 13 is dealt with in detail in Lesson 10, so we will not continue our discussion of it here.

THE PRIORITY OF ORDER IN MINISTRY

Now let's look in detail at chapter 14 as Paul discusses how to exercise spiritual language in a public setting and with control. Look up the following verses in chapter 14 and answer the questions below.

What are the two things that Paul tells the believers to do in verse 14:1?

What spiritual gift does he emphasize? Why (vv. 2–4)?

Does Paul think speaking in tongues is important (vv. 2, 4, 5)?

In those same three verses, what does Paul say speaking in tongues accomplishes?

Why do you think Paul makes a distinction between spiritual language in public and private use (vv. 6–12)?

KINGDOM EXTRA

The sincere Spirit-filled believer will not be preoccupied with this gift of tongues alone, for he sees it as only one of many gifts given for the "wholeness" of the church; therefore, he does not worship or meet with others just to speak in tongues for the mere sake of the practice itself. Such motivation would be immature, vain, and idolatrous. Rather, sincere believers gather to worship God and to be thoroughly equipped for every good work through the teaching of His Word (2 Tim. 3:16, 17).[5] Consequently, the scripturally sensitive believer recognizes that in a group gathering, the exercise of tongues (with interpretation each time, of course) is to be limited to sequences of two or three at the most. While many hold this to be a rigid number, others understand it to be a flexible guideline to keep a worship service in balance.[6]

Is spiritual language inappropriate in a public gathering (v. 12–13)?

In verses 14–19, Paul speaks about both the public and personal use of spiritual language. List what he says for each:

> Public   Personal

What is Paul calling the Corinthians to do in verse 20?

In verses 21–25, Paul makes a comparison between uninterpreted tongues and prophecy in a public gathering. What does he say about each?

What is prophecy to accomplish in the public gathering?

KINGDOM EXTRA

The life of the New Testament church is intended to be blessed by the presence of the gift of prophecy. As Paul states here in noting love as our *primary* pursuit, prophecy is to be welcomed for the "edification and exhortation and comfort" of the congregation—corporately and individually (v. 3). Such encouragement of each other is "prophecy," not "words" in the sense of the Bible, which uses the very words of God, but in the sense of human words the Holy Spirit uniquely brings to mind.

The practice of the gift of prophecy is one purpose of Holy Spirit fullness (Acts 2:17). It also fulfills Joel's prophecy (Joel 2:28) and Moses' earlier expressed hope (Num. 11:29).

The operation of the gift of prophecy is encouraged by Peter (1 Pet. 4:11), and Paul says that it is within the potential of every believer (1 Cor. 14:31). It is intended as a means of broad participation among the congregation, mutually benefiting each other with anointed, loving words of upbuilding, insight, and affirmation. Such prophecy may provide such insight that hearts are humbled in worship of God, suddenly made aware of His Spirit's knowledge of their need and readiness to answer it (1 Cor. 14:24, 25). Prophecy of this order is also a means by which vision and expectation are prompted and provided, and without which people may become passive or neglectful (1 Sam. 3:1; Prov. 29:18; Acts 2:17). There are specific guidelines for the operation of this gift, as with all gifts of the Holy Spirit, to ensure that one gift not supplant the exercise of others or usurp the authority of spiritual leadership. Further, all such prophecy is subordinated to the plumb line of God's Eternal Word, the Bible—the standard by which all prophetic utterance in the church is to be judged (1 Cor. 14:26–33).[7]

In verse 26, Paul turns a corner and begins to discuss order in church meetings. List the regulations he gives for services in each of the following verses.

v. 26

v. 27

What does this verse tell us about the acceptability of giving a tongue in a public gathering? What is the requirement for that to be permitted (v. 28)?

v. 29

v. 30

v. 31

v. 32

What does this tell us about how a prophecy is to be delivered? Is the prophet out of control?

vv. 34, 35

WORD WEALTH

Subject, *hupotasso:* Literally "to stand under." The word suggests subordination, obedience, submission, subservience, subjection. The divine gift of prophetic utterance is put under the control and responsibility of the possessor.[8]

PROBING THE DEPTHS

First Corinthians 14:34, 35 are very difficult and are subject to great debate. The best interpretation is probably to see Paul as not forbidding women to manifest spiritual gifts in the service (see 11:5; Acts 2:18; 21:9). Rather, he prohibits undisciplined discussion that would disturb the service. Also possible is the forbidden speaking along the lines of 1 Tim.

2:11–15, which precludes women from becoming indepen-
dent doctrinal (apostolic) authorities over men. One other
view sees vv. 34, 35 as Paul's quoting from their letter to him
in beginning a new paragraph. Proponents of this view then
see v. 36 as his rhetorical answer, essentially saying, "What?
Men only? Nonsense!" Perhaps more helpful is noting that the
Greek word here for "woman" is also translatable "wife." Thus,
the command may confront the impropriety in any age for a
wife to domineeringly issue doctrinal commands and enforce
authoritative teachings, embarrassing her husband in public.
The Bible does not assign rigid social or church roles to men
and women, but it does place headship and authority in hus-
bands as an abiding principle for this age.[9]

Read verses 36–38. What is Paul trying to communicate here?

Paul gives four final commands in verses 39, 40. What are they?

Throughout this chapter, Paul apparently is equating
"tongues + interpretation" and "prophecy." Do you think this is
an accurate assessment? Which verses seem to say that?

What is the Holy Spirit's basic purpose (1 Cor. 14:26, 40)?

JUDGING PROPHECY

First Corinthians 14:29 makes clear that prophecy is not to
simply be accepted at face value but is to be judged, considered,
weighed, and valued accordingly. Yet at the same time 1 Thessalonians 5:20 warns us not to despise prophesying. So prophecy
isn't to simply be dismissed out of hand either. Look up the following verses and write down what guidelines we can learn to
properly judge prophecy.

Romans 12:6

Ephesians 3:5; 4:11; 5:10

1 Thessalonians 5:21

1 Peter 1:10

2 Peter 2:1; 3:2

1 John 4:1

 KINGDOM EXTRA

Seven Ways That Prophecy Is To Be Kept In Perspective

1. God's Word must always be elevated as the plumb line by which all prophetic utterance is measured.

2. God's Word, the Bible, must always be the focus of our hunger for truth, growth in faith, and guidance for life.

3. Jesus Christ Himself must always be the center of focus; no gift, or its exercise, should be drawing us from Him to focus on a human instrument.

4. All exercise of gifts in a congregation must be in submission to local church eldership, not as a controlling device but as a means of protection, adjustment, and correction.

5. All prophecy should be applied, not merely applauded. The Word of the Holy Spirit is to call us to action, not to entertain or excite us.

6. Personal prophecies should never introduce control or direction over human beings. Christ, not prophets or prophecies, is the Lord of each of His redeemed.

7. Always remember, "we prophesy in part," (1 Cor. 13:9), and therefore no prophecy is a final word on something, nor necessarily to be received as a timeless direction on anything.[10]

Look up the following verses that allude to "personal" prophesies, or prophesies given by one person to another person: Acts 21:10–13; 1 Timothy 1:18; 4:14

KINGDOM EXTRA

The Bible clearly allows for personal prophecy. Nathan brought David a confrontive "word" from God (2 Sam. 12:13); Isaiah predicted Hezekiah's death (Is. 38:1); and in this text Agabus told Paul he faced trouble in Jerusalem. "Personal prophecy" refers to a prophecy ("word") the Holy Spirit may prompt one person to give another, relating to personal matters. Many feel deep reservations about this operation of the gift of prophecy because sometimes it is abused. True "words" may be used to manipulate others, or they may be unwisely or hastily applied. This passage reveals safeguards against abusive uses of personal prophecy, allowing us to implement this biblical practice. First, the "word" will usually not be new to the mind of the person addressed, but it will confirm something God is already dealing with him or her about. From Acts 20:22–24 we know Paul was already sensitive to the issue Agabus raised. Second, the character of the person bringing the "word" ought to be weighed. Agabus's credibility is related not to his claim of having a "word," but to his record as a trustworthy man of God used in the exercise of this gift (11:28; 21:10). Third, remember that the prophecy, or "word," is not to be considered "controlling." In other words, such prophecies should never be perceived as dominating anyone's free will. Christian living is never cultish—governed by omens or the counsel of gurus. Paul did not change his plans because of Agabus's prophecy or because of the urging of others (vv. 12–14); he received the "word" graciously but continued his plans nonetheless. Fourth, all prophecy is "in part" (1 Cor. 13:9), which means that as true as that "part" may be, it does not give the whole picture. Agabus's "word" was true, and Paul was bound in Jerusalem. But this also occasioned an opportunity to eventually minister in Rome (Acts 23:11). Finally, in the light of a "word," we should prayerfully consider the word as Mary did the shepherds' report (Luke 2:19). A hasty response is never required: simply wait on God. We should then move ahead with trust in God, as Hezekiah did. He had been told that he would shortly die; but he prayed, instead of merely surrendering to the prophecy, and his life realized its intended length—unshortened by his diseased condition. Occasional personal prophecy is not risky if kept on biblical footings, but neither is it to become the way we plan or direct our lives.[11]

FAITH ALIVE

How do you feel that Paul's phrase "earnestly desire the best gifts" applies to you?

How do you feel about the idea of the Holy Spirit using you to deliver a gift of the Spirit?

How do you feel about the issue of prophecy?

Have you ever received a personal prophecy?

How did it work out in your life?

How has this study affected your view of a tongue + interpretation or prophecy in the public assembly of believers?

1. *Spirit-Filled Life Bible* (Nashville, TN: Thomas Nelson Publishers, 1991), 1717–1718, "Purpose, Background, Content, and Personal Application of 1 Corinthians."

2. Ibid., 1738–1739, "Textnote: 1 Cor. 12:31."

3. Ibid., 1719, "Word Wealth: 1 Cor. 1:7, gift."

4. Ibid., 1738–1739, "Textnote: 1 Cor. 12:31."

5. Ibid., 2021, "Tongues for Public Exhortation."

6. Ibid., 1742, "Kingdom Dynamics: 1 Cor. 14:27, Limits to Exercising Tongues."

7. Ibid., 1740, "Kingdom Dynamics: 1 Cor. 14:1, The Propriety and Desirability of Prophecy."

8. Ibid., 1742, "Word Wealth: 1 Cor. 14:32, subject."

9. Ibid., 1742, "Textnote: 1 Cor. 14:34, 35."

10. Jack Hayford, *The Beauty of Spiritual Language* (Dallas, TX: Word Publishing, 1992), 128–129.

11. *Spirit-Filled Life Study Bible*, 1668–1669, "Kingdom Dynamics: Acts 21:11, The Issue of Personal Prophecy."

Lesson 9/*Spiritual Prayer in Spiritual Warfare*

Recently my husband decided to fix our bathroom faucet. Now, however loveable he may be, his renown as Mr. Fix-it has become a standing joke in our family because he's hopeless at fixing things! But on this occasion, he thought this was a simple job and was sure he could handle it.

The next thing I heard, as I was working in the kitchen, was loud shouts for help coming from the bathroom. I rushed in, only to see water spraying *everywhere!* Water was hitting the ceiling, drenching the walls, and soaking the hallway carpet! What had started out as a very simple undertaking had become a huge project. Why? Because my husband didn't have the right tools for the job. By contrast, Jesus has provided us with all of the tools we need to live in His kingdom, grow in our walk with Him, and war against the power of darkness! And spiritual language in prayer and song is a principle tool for waging effective warfare (Eph. 6:13, 18).

When Jesus left His disciples to return to heaven, He knew what they would be facing—He had faced Satan personally in His temptation (Luke 4:1–13). Look up the following Scriptures on what we are dealing with in our enemy, the devil: Genesis 3:4, 5; Job 2:7; Zechariah 3:1; Matthew 10:16; 13:19; Luke 22:31; John 8:44; 10:10; 1 Peter 5:8

 KINGDOM EXTRA

As Jesus confronts Satan, He dramatically exposes the Adversary's relationship to this present world. Note the significance in Satan's offer to Jesus of "all the kingdoms of the world" (Luke 4:5, 6). Here we see the Adversary as adminis-trator of the curse on this planet, a role he has held since man's dominion was lost and forfeited at the Fall. Because of this, Jesus does not contest the Devil's right to make that offer of this world's kingdoms and glory, but He pointedly denies the terms for their being gained. Jesus knows He is here to regain and ultimately win them, but He will do so on the Father's terms, not the Adversary's. Still, the present world systems are largely grounded by the limited but powerful and destructive rule of the one Jesus calls "the ruler of this world" (John 12:31; 16:30). Understanding these facts, we are wise not to attribute to God anything of the disorder of our confused, sin-riddled, diseased, tragedy-ridden, and tormented planet. "This present evil age" (Gal. 1:4) "lies *under the sway of* the wicked one" (1 John 5:19). But Jesus also said that Satan's rule "will be cast down," and that he "has nothing in Me," that is, no control over Christ or Christ's own. "He who is in you is greater than he who is in the world" (1 John 4:4).[1]

Jesus knew what we would be facing, but He didn't leave us defenseless—He left us with the right tools or, in this case, the right weapons.

You're in the Army Now

The New Testament repeatedly describes our life in the Spirit in military terms. Look up these Scriptures and write down how Paul describes our struggle against Satan.

Romans 7:23

2 Corinthians 10:4

Ephesians 6:12

1 Timothy 1:18; 6:12

2 Timothy 2:4

Matthew 11:12: Even Jesus, Himself, notwithstanding His mercy toward humanity, taught a spiritually aggressive gospel.

 KINGDOM EXTRA

Jesus asserts the "violence" of the kingdom. The unique grammatical construction of the text does not make clear if the kingdom of God is the victim of violence or if, as the kingdom advances in victory, it does so through violent spiritual conflict and warfare. But the context does. Jesus' references to the nonreligious style of John and the confrontive, miraculous ministry of Elijah teach that the kingdom of God makes its penetration by a kind of violent entry opposing the human status quo. It transcends the softness (Matt. 11:8) of staid religious formalism and exceeds the pretension of child's play (Matt. 11:16, 17). It refuses to "dance to the music" of society's expectation that the religious community provide either entertainment ("we played the flute") or dead traditionalism ("we mourned").

Jesus defines the "violence" of His kingdom's expansion by defining the "sword" and "fire" He has brought as different from the battle techniques of political or military warfare (compare Matt. 10:34–39 and Luke 12:49–53 with John 18:36). The upheaval caused by the kingdom of God is not caused by political provocation or armed advance. It is the result of God's order shaking relationships, households, cities, and nations by the entry of the Holy Spirit's power working in people. (See also Luke 16:16.)[2]

Matthew 16:18, 19; 18:18; 28:18

Perhaps the best-known passage dealing with spiritual warfare is that of Ephesians 6:13–18 where Paul lists our spiritual armor. Read this passage and list the six weapons that have been given to us.

KINGDOM EXTRA

In Ephesians 6:10–18, Paul admonishes us to put on the whole armor of God in order to stand against the forces of hell. It is clear that our warfare is not against physical forces but against invisible powers who have clearly defined levels of authority in a real, though invisible, sphere of activity. Paul, however, not only warns us of a clearly defined structure in the invisible realm, he instructs us to take up the whole armor of God in order to maintain a "battle-stance" against this unseen satanic structure. All of this armor is not just a passive protection in facing the enemy; it is to be used offensively against these satanic forces. Note Paul's final directive: we are to be "praying always with all prayer and supplication in the Spirit" (v. 18). Thus, prayer is not so much a weapon, or even a part of the armor, as it is the means by which we engage in the battle itself and the purpose for which we are armed. To put on the armor of God is to prepare for battle. Prayer is the battle itself, with God's Word being our chief weapon employed against Satan during our struggle.[3]

MARCHING ON OUR KNEES

We will be looking at each piece of armor individually, but let us start by looking at where the battle takes place: in prayer (v. 18). The New Testament puts great emphasis on the prayer of the believer, and here in Ephesians Paul points out the importance of prayer in spiritual warfare. Look up these verses on prayer and write down how they apply to the life of the believer.

Matthew 7:7; 26:41

Luke 18:1

John 16:24

Acts 4:31

KINGDOM EXTRA

Acts 4:1–37 shows us the early church's response when persecutors tried to shut down the Christian movement. They went to prayer! Often the things that threaten to suffocate or destroy the church turn out to be the means of its preservation and advance. This persecution was sparked by controversy over a miracle, just as skeptics still debate the relationship of miracles to Christianity. These early believers knew that if it could be established that the lame man's healing had been accomplished in the name and power of Jesus, Christ's power and authority would be clearly confirmed. Therefore, they went to prayer. The results? Great grace and boldness. Great power and unity (vv. 32–34). They teach us the pathway to proving the reality of our faith: not debate or argument, but prayer.[4]

Romans 12:12

1 Corinthians 7:5

Philippians 4:6

Colossians 4:2, 12

1 Thessalonians 3:10; 5:17

How do you think that spiritual language would help the believer to obey Paul's command in 1 Thessalonians 5:17?

1 Timothy 2:1, 8; 4:5

James 5:13, 14

1 Peter 3:7; 4:7

Jude 20

Revelation 5:8; 8:3

The power of our prayer is that in it we are seeking God's will, not our own. That means that into any and every situation we face, we are establishing—or claiming territory, as the explorers of old—God's kingdom rule through prayer.

 KINGDOM EXTRA

Children of God may have **confidence** of free access and boldness of speech in presenting their requests to Him. There is, however, a limitation to the assurance that our prayers will be answered. The New Testament elsewhere bases the assurance on asking in Jesus' name (John 14:13, 14; 15:16; 16:23, 24), abiding in Christ and allowing His words to abide in us (John 15:7), having faith (Matt. 21:22; James 1:6), and being righteous in life and fervent in prayer (1 John 3:21, 22; James 5:16). In 1 John 5:14, 15, John says that we must ask **according to His will,** which inclusively states the fundamental condition for assurance in prayer. One who abides in Christ and whose words abide in him; who prays in the name of Jesus, that is, in accord with His character and nature; and who is full of faith and righteousness is not inclined to pray anything contrary to His will. But more than *how* we pray, God wills and cares *that* we pray. Genuine prayer is not an attempt at precise means of getting God to meet our desires and demands; but rather, in subordinating our will to His, we open the doorway to His fullest blessings being released in our lives.[5]

Look up these verses about seeking God's will first: Psalm 143:10; Matthew 6:10, 33; John 7:17

KINGDOM EXTRA

In Luke 16:16, Jesus declares the advance of the kingdom of God is the result of two things: <u>preaching</u> and <u>pressing in</u>. He shows the gospel of the kingdom must be proclaimed with spiritual passion. In every generation believers have to determine whether they will respond to this truth with sensible minds and sensitive hearts. To overlook it will bring a passivity that limits the ministry of God's kingdom to extending the terms of truth and love—that is, teaching or educating and engaging in acts of kindness. Without question, we must do these things. However, apart from 1) an impassioned pursuit of prayer, 2) confrontation with the demonic, 3) expectation of the miraculous, and 4) a burning heart for evangelism, the kingdom of God makes little penetration in the world.

At the same time, overstatement of "pressing" is likely to produce rabid fanatics who justify any behavior in Jesus' name as applying the boldness spoken of here. Such travesties in church history as the Crusades and various efforts at politicizing in a quest to produce righteousness in society through Earth-level rule are extremes we must learn to reject. "Pressing in" is accomplished first in prayer warfare, coupled with a will to surrender one's life and self-interests, in order to gain God's kingdom goals.[6]

Earlier we looked up Matthew 18:19. Look it up again and copy it here:

How would you describe the connection between this verse and the verses you just looked up on seeking God's will first?

 KINGDOM EXTRA

Matthew 16:19 says that Jesus "will give you the keys of the kingdom of heaven, and whatever you bind on earth will be bound in heaven, and whatever you loose on earth will be

loosed in heaven." The implications of this significant verse are diverse and need to be understood. Jesus' terminology has elements of symbolism and entails a complex Greek construction; therefore, different interpretations are viable.

Keys denote authority. Through Peter, a representative of the church throughout the ages, Jesus is passing on to His church His authority or control to **bind** and to **loose on earth**. The Greek construction behind **will be bound** and **will be loosed** indicates that Jesus is the One who has activated the provisions through His Cross; the church is then charged with implementation of what He has released through His life, death, and Resurrection.

Clearly rabbinic in imagery, binding and loosing have to do with forbidding or permitting. In other words, Jesus is stating that the church will be empowered to continue in the privileged responsibility of leavening the earth with His kingdom power and provision. For example, if someone is bound by sin, the church can "loose" him by preaching the provision of freedom from sin in Jesus Christ (Rom. 6:14). If someone is indwelt by a demon, the church can "bind" the demon by commanding its departure (Acts 16:18), realizing that Jesus alone made this provision possible (Matt. 12:29). How the church binds and looses is diverse and would most certainly extend far beyond the mere use of these terms in prayerful petitions.[7]

While Jesus began teaching His disciples about the authority He was giving them, the victory was not fully realized until the Cross. Look up these verses on our authority in Christ: Luke 10:19; 1 Corinthians 15:24; Ephesians 1:20–22; 2:6. Where are we seated? Colossians 2:10, 13–15

 KINGDOM EXTRA

Colossians 2:13–15 tells us that Jesus Christ's triumph over sin and evil powers was accomplished in "it"—that is, in the Cross. This text, joined to and studied beside others (Eph. 2:13–16; Gal. 3:13, 14; 2 Cor. 5:14–17; Rom. 5:6–15; and Rev. 12:10, 11), firmly establishes Jesus' suffering, shed blood, sacrificial death, and resurrection triumph as the only adequate and available ground for ransom from sin, reconcili-

ation to God, redemption from slavery, and restoration. The Cross is the sole hope and means for full reinstatement to relationship with God and rulership under Him—to "reign in life" (Rom. 5:17). To avoid presumption or imbalance regarding the message and ministry of the present power of the kingdom of God, we must focus on and regularly review two points; the source and the grounds for the delegation of such authority and power. 1) God's sovereign authority and almighty power is the source from which mankind derives any ability to share in the exercise of God's kingdom power. 2) But even more important, seeing sinful, fallen man had lost all claim to his early privilege of rulership under God, let us remember the <u>grounds</u> upon which all kingdom privilege or power may be restored and by which such spiritual ministry with authority may be exercised.[8]

Before we look at the other spiritual weapons listed in Ephesians 6, let's reassess the two main facts we've discussed so far:

1. Our authority is in the power of Jesus' _____.

2. The spiritual battle takes place primarily through_____.

THE WEAPONS OF OUR WARFARE

Now that we've taken a look at where the battle takes place, let's go back to verse 14 and look at our six weapons: truth, righteousness, the gospel of peace, faith, salvation, and the Word of God.

Truth

"Truth" is basic to everything that we put our faith in as believers. God is truth, truth came to us through Jesus, the Holy Spirit guides us into truth, the Word is truth, and God calls us to live in truth as we become more like Him. Look up the following verses that describe the truth of God: Exodus 34:6; Deuteronomy 32:4; Psalm 33:4; 100:5; John 1:17; 14:6

Read the following Scriptures and write down what our response is to be to truth and how we are to include it in our lives.

1 Samuel 12:24

Psalm 25:5; Psalm 51:6

Ephesians 4:15

Read Psalm 86:11 and Proverbs 8:7. These verses seem to imply that living in truth is a choice. What do you think?

   KINGDOM EXTRA

Truth, *'emet* (Hebrew) and *aletheia* (Greek): *'Emet* derives from the verb *'aman,* meaning "to be firm, permanent, and established." *'Emet* conveys a sense of dependability, firmness, and reliability. Truth is therefore something upon which a person may confidently stake his life.[9] *Aletheia* is derived from negative, *a,* and *lanthano,* "to be hidden," "to escape notice." *Aletheia* is the opposite of fictitious, feigned, or false. It denotes veracity, reality, sincerity, accuracy, integrity, truthfulness, dependability, and propriety.[10]

Look up the following verses and write down how truth relates to spiritual warfare and how it functions as a weapon on our behalf.

Psalm 91:4

Proverbs 12:19

Proverbs 20:28

John 8:32

Righteousness
   Look up these verses and write down how righteousness can be 1) a weapon *against* the enemy, and 2) a protection *from* the enemy.

Deuteronomy 16:19

How might the commands in this verse help us in waging spiritual warfare?

What does honesty have to do with spiritual warfare?

Psalm 5:12; 34:19

Psalm 37:39

Psalm 92:15; 118:15; 140:13

Psalm 142:7: What does this verse tell us about waging spiritual warfare alone?

Proverbs 12:3; 15:28; 28:1

Jeremiah 11:20

Luke 1:6

2 Thessalonians 1:6

James 5:16

1 Peter 3:12

Now look up these verses and write down some of God's promises to His righteous ones.

Job 36:7

Psalm 37:25; 92:12; 97:11

Isaiah 33:15, 16

Matthew 5:6

2 Corinthians 9:10

1 John 1:9

The Gospel of Peace

Jesus, Himself, defined what His gospel was all about. Look up Luke 4:18, 19 and copy Jesus' definition of the gospel.

In Ephesians 6, Paul describes the gospel as a gospel of *peace*. Does "peace" describe Jesus' gospel? How?

WORD WEALTH

Peace, *eirene:* A state of rest, quietness, and calmness; an absence of strife; tranquility. It generally denotes a perfect well-being. *Eirene* includes harmonious relationships between God and men, men and men, nations, and families. Jesus as Prince of Peace gives peace to those who call upon Him for personal salvation.[11]

Look up these verses and write down what Scripture tells us about peace.

Psalm 29:11; 85:10

What do you think the latter verse tells us about the interaction of the weapons of righteousness and peace?

Proverbs 3:13, 17

Ecclesiastes 3:8

How might this apply to the subject of spiritual warfare? (See also Rom. 16:20.)

John 16:33

1 Corinthians 14:33

Colossians 1:20

Write down *why* we can have peace.

The following verses tell us what we can do to have peace. Look up these verses and write down what those things are:

Psalm 34:14; 119:165

Proverbs 12:20

Isaiah 26:3

Look up this next set of verses and write down what it says peace has to do with the preaching of the gospel:

Nahum 1:15; Romans 10:15

Zechariah 9:9, 10

Acts 10:36

Ephesians 2:17

Faith
     Look up the following verses and write down what they tell us about faith.

Matthew 9:29; 17:20

Mark 9:23; 11:22

Acts 26:18

Romans 10:17

What do we need to hear for faith to come?

Romans 11:20; Hebrews 11:6; James 2:18

How do you think faith is shown in spiritual warfare?

(For more on "faith," see Lesson 10.)

Salvation
   Scripture teaches that we can never save ourselves. Look up these verses and write down where our salvation comes from.

Exodus 14:13

Psalm 3:8; 68:20; 118:14

Habakkuk 3:18

Acts 4:12

Romans 1:16

Titus 2:11

1 Peter 1:10

   Scripture also promises that when we accept Jesus Christ and His offer of salvation, He makes us completely new. Look up these verses that tell us about the newness of life offered to us in Christ: Ezekiel 11:19; 2 Corinthians 4:16; 5:17; Galatians 6:15; Ephesians 2:15; 4:24; Colossians 3:9, 10

The following verses tell us about the newness of *mind* that Jesus makes possible: Romans 12:2; 1 Corinthians 2:16; Ephesians 4:23; Philippians 2:5; 2 Timothy 1:7; Hebrews 8:10; 1 Peter 1:13

What significance is there between the *helmet* of salvation and our newness of mind?

How do you think your thought life might affect you in the midst of spiritual battle?

Write out 1 Thessalonians 5:23 as a reminder that our salvation is to affect every part of our being.

The Word of God
The Word of God has been given to us as a sword to slice through every lie of the Adversary. That shouldn't be surprising since the basic attribute of Scripture is truth (John 17:17). Let's start our overview of the use of Scripture in spiritual warfare by looking at the temptation of Jesus. Read Luke 4:1–13 and answer the following questions.

How did Jesus fight each temptation?

What does this say to us about the use of the Word in the midst of spiritual warfare?

Luke 4:13, says that the devil departed from Jesus until when?

What does this verse say about *when* the devil chooses to tempt us?

Look up these other verses about the Word of God and write down what you can learn about the power of God's Word from each one.

Jeremiah 5:14; Mark 14:49; Ephesians 5:26; Philippians 2:16; Colossians 3:16; 2 Timothy 3:16, 17; Hebrews 4:12; 1 Peter 1:23; 2 Peter 1:20, 21; 3:5; Revelation 19:13

 FAITH ALIVE

Write out Ephesians 6:13.

What does this mean to you personally?

How do you think you "take up the whole armor of God" daily?

What area of your life needs to be dealt with through spiritual warfare?

What steps do you feel you need to take in pursuing freedom in Christ?

Is there a trustworthy, mature believer in your life who would stand with you in prayer?

Stop right now and ask the Lord:
1) To bring freedom to this area of your life.
2) To help you stand strong in the power of *His* might.
3) To give you faith to see the battle to its end.
4) To provide you with strong support from other believers.

1. *Spirit-Filled Life Bible* (Nashville, TN: Thomas Nelson Publishers, 1991), 1517, "Kingdom Dynamics: Luke 4:14–32, Earth's Evil 'Ruler.'"

2. Ibid., 1424, "Kingdom Dynamics: Matt. 11:12, Taking It by Force."

3. Ibid., 1797, "Kingdom Dynamics: Eph. 6:10–18, Spiritual Warfare."

4. Ibid., 1630–1631, "Kingdom Dynamics: Acts 4:1–37, Prayer, the Proving Grounds of Our Faith."

5. Ibid., 1934, "Textnotes: 1 John 5:14, 15."

6. Ibid., 1547, "Kingdom Dynamics: Luke 16:16, Pressing In."

7. Ibid., 1436, "Textnotes: Matt. 16:19."

8. Ibid., 1816–1817, "Kingdom Dynamics: Col. 2:13–15, Grounds of Authority."

9. Ibid., 774, "Word Wealth: Ps. 25:5, truth."

10. Ibid., 1580, "Word Wealth: John 4:24, truth."

11. Ibid., 1510, "Word Wealth: Luke 1:79, peace."

Lesson 10/ "A More Excellent Way"

Grace is a friend of mine whose father-in-law would often say to her husband, "Make sure you tell your wife you love her every day!" He would then turn to Grace and demand to know, "Is he telling you he loves you every day?"

After decades of marriage, Grace's father-in-law knew something that Grace and her husband had yet to learn: love, and the ongoing expression of it, is crucial for the health of a relationship. The same is true of our spiritual relationships: nurturing our love toward the Father, growing in our love toward one another, and enlarging our awareness of God's love toward us. God tells us He loves us . . . every day and in every circumstance. His love not only saves us from sin, but Romans 5:5 establishes the fact that it is the Holy Spirit's work in our lives that pours the love of God into our hearts. As we open to broader dimensions of the Holy Spirit's work in our lives, we also open to the outpouring of God's ever-expanding love into our hearts.

LOVE DIVINE, ALL LOVE EXCELLING

The story of God's redemptive love is most clearly and simply seen in the well-known verse, John 3:16. Look up this Scripture and write it out. Circle the word that describes how God feels about us.

 WORD WEALTH

Loved, *agapao:* Unconditional love, love by choice and by an act of the will. The word denotes unconquerable benevolence and undefeatable goodwill. *Agapao* will never seek anything but the highest good for fellow mankind. *Agapao* (the verb) and *agape* (the noun) are the words for God's unconditional love. It does not need a chemistry, an affinity, or a feeling. *Agapao* is a word that exclusively belongs to the Christian community. It is a love virtually unknown to writers outside the New Testament.[1]

 KINGDOM EXTRA

Upon repentance, a new order of life opens to the believer in Jesus Christ. Jesus used the figure of "new birth" to dramatically indicate three things: 1) Without New Birth, there is no life and no relationship with God (14:6). 2) In New Birth, new perspective comes as we "see the kingdom of God" (3:3), God's Word becomes clear, and the Holy Spirit's works and wonders are believed and experienced—faith is alive. 3) Through New Birth we are introduced—literally we "enter" (v. 5)—to a new realm, where God's new kingdom order can be realized (2 Cor. 5:17). New Birth is more than simply being "saved." It is a requalifying experience, opening up the possibilities of our whole being to the supernatural dimension of life and fitting us for a beginning in God's kingdom order.[2]

Throughout Scripture, we see the love of God consistently and continually drawing people back to Him. Look up these verses and write down how God's love is shown to us.

Deuteronomy 7:8, 13; Psalm 91:14; Isaiah 63:9; Jeremiah 31:3; Hosea 3:1; 11:4; Zephaniah 3:17; John 14:23; 15:9; Romans 5:8; Ephesians 2:4, 5; 5:2, 25; 1 John 3:1; 4:10; Revelation 1:5

Scripture also says that we are to have that same love of God manifest in our own lives. Look up Galatians 5:22 and list the fruit of the Spirit that God wants to grow in us.

Now look up these verses and write down *how* Christ's love is to be shown in our lives.
Leviticus 19:18

Deuteronomy 6:5; 10:19; 11:1

Psalm 5:11; 97:10

Proverbs 10:12

Micah 6:8

Matthew 5:43, 44; Luke 10:27

John 13:35; 14:21

Romans 12:9, 10; 13:10

Galatians 5:6, 13; Ephesians 4:15; Philippians 1:9; Colossians 2:2; 1 Thessalonians 1:3

1 Peter 2:17; 1 John 2:5; 3:18; 4:17, 18

KINGDOM EXTRA

John 15:12, 13 summarizes the entire duty and direction of the disciple of Jesus. The direct simplicity of this statement establishes the priority and the pathway we are to pursue. 1) Our priority is to love one another. 2) Our pathway is to love as Christ loved us, "laying down His life." Who can measure this love? Christ gave up the comforts, joys, and adoration of heaven to be sullied by the soil of Earth and to carry the sins of sinners. His bearing of agonizing pain through beatings, nails in His hands, the spear in His side, the thorns on His head, all exemplify the measure of His love. We find His love, but we also see His manner of loving and are called to bear with others' sins, with inflicted pain, with stabbing, cruel remarks and treatment. Impossible? Yes, to human nature; but as new temples of the Holy Spirit, who has poured out the love of God into our hearts, we can ask for and receive the grace and guidance to love as Jesus loved.[3]

KINGDOM EXTRA

In Second Peter 1, Peter describes God's "great and precious promises" (v. 4) intended to enable us 1) to be "partakers" in His divine nature and 2) to allow us to "escape the corruption *that is* in the world." These graces are necessary to lift us above the decay of human nature and unto "brotherly kindness" and "love" (v. 7). Brotherly kindness dissolves personal infighting and ungracious ignoring of one another. It allows refocusing on our real enemy—Satan. Further, to master love is to receive and release *agape* love: that Christlike, unconditional gift that is full of affection, bursting with benevolence, and that provides a love feast to all to whom we minister in the name of Jesus. This text is a promise for those yielded enough to let these gifts flow: we can actually participate in the divine nature of God, which is elevated above the corrupt, divisive spirit of the world.[4]

Scripture also gives us promises of what will happen in our lives if we love and serve God. Look up these verses and write down what is promised to us.

Deuteronomy 5:8–10 (note v. 10)

Judges 5:31; Psalm 145:20; Proverbs 8:21; Romans 8:28

WORD WEALTH

Good, *agathos:* Good, in a physical and moral sense, and which produces benefits. The word is used of persons, things, acts, conditions, and so on. A synonym of *agathos* is *kalos,* good in an aesthetic sense, suggesting attractiveness, excellence.[5]

> 1 Corinthians 2:9
> James 1:12

KINGDOM EXTRA

In Genesis 12:1–3, God promises to make Abraham great; and God did bless Abraham in many ways, including material blessing. See 13:1, 2, where we see how Abraham was made very rich. See also 24:35, where Abraham's servant reports that "the Lord has blessed my master greatly," and then enumerates the material blessings that God had given to Abraham. The dynamic of this historic fact becomes pertinent to every believer today.

In Galatians 3:13, 14, God promises to give all believers the blessings of Abraham, telling us that Jesus became a curse for us so that we might receive "the blessings of Abraham." This begins, of course, with our being born again, or becoming new creatures in Christ Jesus. But "the blessings of Abraham" involve other things as well. The Lord wants us to prosper—spiritually, emotionally and physically, and materially. The blessings are ours by His promise, and we need make no apology for the fact that prosperity is included.[6]

Before we move on to set spiritual language in the context of love, let's look at one more promise that is ours through the love of God: He will not be separated from us. Read Romans 8:35–39. List all of the things that God's love is able to overcome:

THE LANGUAGE OF LOVE

First Corinthians 13 has been called "The Love Chapter" of Scripture. It has been read at weddings and considered a classic piece of poetry in literature. But in the context of Scripture, Paul places it directly between the two chapters that deal with the use of spiritual language in both public and private practice. Compare 1 Corinthians 12:31; 13:13; and 14:1. Why do you think Paul deals with the subject of love here, in the midst of his discourse on spiritual language?

Based on these Scriptures, what conclusions would you draw about how spiritual language is to be used?

   KINGDOM EXTRA

A more excellent way is not a negative comparison between gifts and love, since the temporal adverb **yet** indicates the continuation of the subject. All manifestations of the Spirit must at the same time manifest the ways of love, for love is the ultimate issue behind all things.[7]

The basis of all gifts is love. *Love,* not the experience of a gift, is the qualifying factor for those who would exercise spiritual gifts. Thus, in the administration of spiritual authority in the local congregation, the Word demands that we "judge" (1 Cor. 14:29) to confirm that those who exercise gifts actually do "pursue love, and desire spiritual *gifts*" (1 Cor. 13:1–13; 14:1).[8]

In 1 Corinthians 13, Paul explains the absolute necessity of **love** (vv. 1–3); defines the essence of love in fourteen of its characteristics (vv. 4–7); and contrasts the eternal perfections of love with the temporal imperfections of gifts (vv. 8–13).[9]

Read 1 Corinthians 13:1-3 and answer the following questions.
How do these three Scriptures specifically address the issue of spiritual language?

What are the three actions of ministry that Paul writes about (one per verse)?

What do we become if we don't minister in love (one per verse)?

Read 1 Corinthians 13:4–7 and write down the fourteen characteristics of love that Paul lists.
v. 4

v. 5

v. 6

v. 7

KINGDOM EXTRA

Love suffers long, having patience with imperfect people. Love **is kind**, active in doing good. **Love does not envy**; since it is nonpossessive and noncompetitive, it actually wants other people to get ahead. Hence it **does not parade itself**. Love has a self-effacing quality; it is not ostentatious. Love **is not puffed up**, treating others arrogantly; it **does not behave rudely**, but displays good manners and courtesy. Love **does not seek its own**, insisting on its own rights and demanding precedence; rather, it is unselfish. Love **is not provoked**; it is not irritable or touchy, rough or hostile, but is graceful under pressure. Love **thinks no evil**; it does not keep an account of wrongs done to it: instead, it erases resentments. Love **does not rejoice in iniquity**, finding satisfaction in the shortcomings of others and spreading an evil report; rather, it **rejoices in the truth**, aggressively advertising the good. Love **bears all things**, defending and holding other people up. Love **believes** the best about others, credits them with good intentions, and is not suspicious. Love **hopes all things**, never giving up on people, but affirming their future. Love **endures all things**, persevering and remaining loyal to the end.[10]

Now read 1 Corinthians 13:8–13 and answer the questions.

What does this passage of Scripture say about prophecy? What does this tell us about the gifts of the Spirit?

What is "that which is perfect"?

KINGDOM EXTRA

That which is perfect refers to the completion of God's purposes after the coming of the Lord Jesus Christ (Rom. 8:18, 19). There is no reason other than human opinion to presume to attribute this reference to the conclusion of the canon of the Scriptures. While the inspired Word of God was completed at the end of the first century, its completion did not signal an end to the continuing operation of the very powers it describes. Rather, that Word instructs us to welcome the Holy Spirit's gifts and ministries in our lives, to round out our sufficiency for ministry to a needy world—through the Word *preached* and the Word *confirmed*.[11]

What do you think verses 11 and 12 are referring to?

In verse 13, Paul writes that the "greatest" attribute is love. Why do you think this is so?

Why do you think it is so important to minister all of the spiritual gifts in the spirit of love?

 KINGDOM EXTRA

The virtues of **faith, hope**, and **love** are necessary in this age; but in the age to come, faith will give way to sight—as in verse 12 where we will "see face to face" (see also 2 Cor. 5:7), and hope will turn into experience—as in verse 11 where the hope of childhood gives way to the greater experience of adulthood (see also Rom. 8:24). Love alone is eternal, for God is love (1 John 4:8).[12]

THE FRUIT OF LOVE

Growth in the Spirit is to be a fact of our lives. Scripture tells us we are to be "rooted and grounded in love" (Eph. 3:17), "grow up in all things unto Him" (Eph. 4:15), and we are to bear fruit (Gal. 5:22, 23). Jesus used the metaphor of Him being the vine and us being the branches (John 15:5). He is our Source for *everything*, and we become more and more like Him in this spiritual growth process.

KINGDOM EXTRA

Being filled with the Spirit calls us as much to character as it does to charismatic activity. The Holy Spirit's fruit is to be grown in our lives every bit as much as His gifts may be shown through us.[13]

Look up the following verses and write down what they tell us about becoming like the One who is our Source.

Leviticus 11:44; Romans 8:29; 2 Corinthians 3:18; Philippians 2:5; 1 Peter 2:21; 2 Peter 1:4; 1 John 3:2

What do these verses tell us?

If we are to continually grow to be like the Father, what should become *our* main attribute (see 1 John 4:8)?

 KINGDOM EXTRA

Before Jesus' death, He gave His disciples the "new commandment"—love one another (John 13:34, 35). That Christ would command us to love indicates that love is not just a feeling or a preference; it is what one does and how he or she relates to others—a decision, a commitment, or a way of behaving. Jesus states that the world will know that we are His disciples if we behave lovingly toward one another. Schisms, disputes, unkind criticisms, and defamation of character are contrary to the spirit of Christ. His love was a sacrificial love. It was unconditional love. His love is constant and self-sustaining. His love provides for the best interests of the beloved, and He commands that we should love one another as He has loved us.[14]

Let's look closer at the fourteen characteristics of love we discovered in 1 Corinthians 13. Look up the following Scriptures and write down what they tell us about each characteristic. **"Love suffers long" (patience):** Psalm 37:7; Ecclesiastes 7:8; Romans 12:9, 12; 15:5; 1 Thessalonians 5:14; 1 Timothy 6:11; Hebrews 6:12; James 1:3, 4; 5:7, 8 Revelation 14:12

Love "is kind" (kindness):

 WORD WEALTH

Kindness, *chrestotes:* Goodness in action, sweetness of disposition, gentleness in dealing with others, benevolence, kindness, affability. The word describes the ability to act for the welfare of those taxing your patience. The Holy Spirit removes abrasive qualities from the character of one under His control.[15]

Proverbs 19:22; 31:26: Describe what you think the "law of kindness" might involve?

Luke 6:35; Ephesians 4:32; Colossians 3:12; 2 Peter 1:5–8

"Does not envy" (contentment): Job 5:2; Proverbs 14:30; Luke 3:14; Galatians 5:26; Philippians 4:11; 1 Timothy 6:6–8; Hebrews 13:5; James 3:16

"Does not parade itself" (modesty):

Luke 20:46: How were the Pharisees parading themselves? What was Jesus warning us about?

Romans 12:3

KINGDOM EXTRA

Because the Bible teaches that human beings are made in God's image, we are to respect the position of each individual under God. This text does not teach that believers should think of themselves as worthless or insignificant beings, but rather that none should consider himself to be more worthy, more important, more deserving of salvation, or more essential than anyone else. Possession of different talents or gifts does not denote differences in worth, for all belong to the one body, to one another, and all are interdependent (Rom. 12:4, 5). To think otherwise is to distort reality. Each individual has intrinsic value and worth, as we are all equal before God and in Christ.[16]

Philippians 4:5; 1 Timothy 2:9: Do you think this verse is speaking only of the way we are to dress? Why or why not?

Titus 2:6: How is "modesty" shown by our "sober-mindedness"?

1 Peter 3:1, 2

"Not puffed up" (humility): Psalm 147:6; Proverbs 13:10; 22:4; 29:23; Isaiah 57:15; Zephaniah 2:3; Matthew 18:4; Romans 12:16; James 4:10; 1 Peter 5:5, 6

"Does not behave rudely" (gracious): Psalm 86:15; Proverbs 11:16; Ecclesiastes 10:12; Luke 4:22; Acts 4:33; Romans 1:5; Ephesians 4:7; Colossians 4:6; 2 Timothy 2:1; 1 Peter 2:3

"Does not seek its own" (unselfish): Acts 4:32–35; Romans 12:10; 15:1, 2; 1 Corinthians 10:24, 33; Galatians 6:2; Philippians 2:4

"Is not provoked" (peaceful): Matthew 5:9; Romans 8:6; 12:18; 2 Corinthians 13:11; Colossians 3:15; 1 Thessalonians 5:13; Hebrews 12:14; James 3:17, 18; 1 Peter 3:11

"Thinks no evil" (pure): Proverbs 15:26; 22:11

 WORD WEALTH

In the New Testament, three different words are translated "pure" and each supplies us with insight on different
aspects of purity in Christ. *Katharos* means without blemish,
clean, undefiled, pure. The word describes physical cleanliness
(Matt. 23:26; 27:59); ceremonial purity (Luke 11:41; Rom.
14:20); and ethical purity (John 13:10; Acts 18:6). Sin pollutes
and defiles, but the blood of Jesus washes the stains away.[17]
Eilikrines literally means "tested by sunlight." The
thought is that of judging something by sunlight to expose any
flaws. The word describes metals with alloys and liquids
unadulterated with foreign substances. In the New Testament
it is used in an ethical and moral sense, free from falsehood,
pure, and without hidden motives. It is a picture of how Jesus
shines the light of His glory into our lives to expose impurities
and cleanse us.[18]
Hagnos comes from the same root as *hagios*, "holy."
The adjective describes a person or thing as clean, modest,
pure, undefiled, morally faultless, and without blemish.
Christ's ability to overcome temptation and remain pure
makes Him a role model for all believers.[19]

Matthew 5:8; Philippians 4:8; 1 Timothy 5:22; 1 Peter 1:22;
2 Peter 3:1; 1 John 3:3

"Not rejoice in iniquity, but rejoices in the truth" (truthful):
John 4:24; 16:13; Ephesians 4:25; 5:9; 1 John 3:18, 19; 4:6; 2
John 1, 23; John 3, 4

"Bears all things" (supporting): 1 Samuel 30:6; Acts 20:35; Romans 14:19; 15:1, 2; 1 Corinthians 8:1; Ephesians 4:29; 1 Thessalonians 5:11

"Believes the best" (faith-filled):

WORD WEALTH

Believe, *pisteuo:* The verb form of *pistis,* "faith." It means to trust in, have faith in, be fully convinced of, acknowledge, rely on. *Pisteuo* is more than credence in church doctrines or articles of faith. It expresses reliance upon and a personal trust that produces obedience. It includes submission and a positive confession of the lordship of Jesus.[20]

Habakkuk 2:4 (See also Rom. 1:17; Gal. 3:11; Heb. 10:38); Luke 17:5, 6; Acts 15:8, 9; Romans 10:17; 1 Corinthians 16:13; 2 Corinthians 5:7; Colossians 2:7; 1 Timothy 6:12; Hebrews 11:1; James 1:3; 3 John 5

"Hopes all things" (hopeful):

WORD WEALTH

Hope, *elpis:* Hope, not in the sense of an optimistic out-look or wishful thinking without any foundation, but in the sense of confident expectation based on solid certainty. Biblical hope rests on God's promises, particularly those pertaining to Christ's return. So certain is the future of the redeemed that the New Testament sometimes speaks of future events in the past tense, as though they were already accomplished. Hope is never inferior to faith, but is an extension of faith. Faith is the present possession of grace; hope is confidence in grace's future accomplishment.[21]

Proverbs 10:28; Zechariah 9:12; Romans 5:5; Galatians 5:5; Colossians 1:27; Titus 2:13; Hebrews 3:6; 1 Peter 3:15

"Endures all things" (persevering):

WORD WEALTH

Endurance, *hupomone:* Constancy, perseverance, continuance, bearing up, steadfastness, holding out, patient endurance. The word combines *hupo,* "under," and *mone,* "to remain." It describes the capacity to continue to bear up under difficult circumstances, not with a passive complacency, but with a hopeful fortitude that actively resists weariness and defeat.[22]

Job 17:9; Romans 5:3, 4; 1 Corinthians 15:58; Galatians 6:9; Ephesians 6:18; 1 Thessalonians 5:21; Hebrews 10:23, 36; 12:1; 1 Peter 1:13; 2 Peter 3:17; Revelation 3:10

FAITH ALIVE

After studying the characteristics of love, we all see areas of our own lives that need growth! But remember—growth is to be a fact of our spiritual life. As you answer the following questions, be as specific as possible.

What characteristic(s) do you feel are most lacking in your life?

Write down how you would like love to be more manifest in your life in the following areas:

your home:

your job/school:

your relationships:

your ministry:

What promises has the Lord given you about these areas of your life? (Remember, the Lord never speaks to us through condemnation. If that's how you feel right now, rebuke the devil and listen to what Jesus has to say about your situation.)

Come to the Lord *right now.* He is the Lord of love and therefore is the only One who can cause love to grow in our lives. Present all areas of your life to Him and ask Him to help you let His love be seen in you.

1. *Spirit-Filled Life Bible* (Nashville, TN: Thomas Nelson Publishers, 1991), 1578, "Word Wealth: John 3:16, loved."

2. Ibid., 1577, "Kingdom Dynamics: John 3:1–5, New Birth."

3. Ibid., 1604, "Kingdom Dynamics: John 15:12, 13, The Priority and Pathway of Brotherly Love."

4. Ibid., 1919, "Kingdom Dynamics: 2 Pet. 1:7, 8, Brotherly Love Flows from the Divine Nature."

5. Ibid., 1802, "Word Wealth: Phil. 1:6, good."

6. Ibid., 22, "Kingdom Dynamics: Gen. 12:1–3, God's Heart to Prosper His People."

7. Ibid., 1738–1739, "Text note on 1 Cor. 12:31."

8. Ibid., 2022, "Holy Spirit Gifts and Power: Tongues for Public Exhortation, #4."

9. Ibid., 1739, "Text note on 1 Cor. 13:1–13."

10. Ibid., 1739, "Text note on 1 Cor. 13:4–7."

11. Ibid., 1739, "Text note on 1 Cor. 13:10."

12. Ibid., 1740, "Text note on 1 Cor. 13:13."

13. Ibid., 1780, "Kingdom Dynamics: Gal. 5:22, 23, A Call to Character."

14. Ibid., 1601, "Kingdom Dynamics: John 13:34, 35, Love—The Testing of Discipleship."

15. Ibid., 1780, "Word Wealth: Gal. 5:22, kindness."

16. Ibid., 1708, "Kingdom Dynamics: Rom. 12:3–5, One Should Not Think Too Highly of Himself."

17. Ibid., 1411, "Word Wealth: Matt. 5:8, pure."

18. Ibid., 1922, "Word Wealth: 2 Pet. 3:1, pure."

19. Ibid., 1930, "Word Wealth: 1 John 3:3, pure."

20. Ibid., 1704, "Word Wealth: Rom. 10:9, believe."

21. Ibid., 1826, "Word Wealth: 1 Thess. 1:3, hope."

22. Ibid., 1884; "Word Wealth: Heb. 10:36, endurance."

Lesson 11/Questions about Spiritual Language

This Lesson is in response to the many questions which plague people about tongues. Often the questions are present as a result of theological systems people have learned which preclude the possibility of the use of tongues in the church today. Others are vexed by doubts concerning their experience because of the way they were ministered to when they received their spiritual language. Still others are simply ignorant of what the Bible says so they struggle with the subject. And finally, there are those who have sought the baptism with the Holy Spirit and have not yet spoken with tongues. This can often be a painful and frustrating experience which wearies the soul and casts doubt on a person's sense of worthiness before God.

THEOLOGICAL CHALLENGES TO SPIRITUAL LANGUAGE

Q: First Corinthians 13:8 declares that tongues will cease. Did tongues stop after the apostles established the church in the first century?

A: First Corinthians 13:8 also declares that prophecies and knowledge will also stop. However, neither have been identified as stopping with the end of the first century. The issue revolves around verse 10, "when the perfect shall come." Dispensational Bible teachers have declared the "perfect" as being the canon of Scripture (our complete Bible as we know it today), and the canon was completed about A.D. 100. This could not have possibly been in the apostle Paul's mind. He had no idea he was writing the Bible at the time he composed the letter to the Corinthians. The "perfect" has historically been judged as being Jesus Christ when He returns for His church.[1]

Q: Doesn't the Bible say that "tongues are the least of the gifts"?

A: No. In 1 Corinthians 12:10, tongues are listed eighth in a group of nine works or gifts of the Holy Spirit. Any value judgment of the gifts is pure human bias. If that were true, the same logic could be applied to 1 Corinthians 13:13. Is love to be the "least" because it is listed last? Of course not!

Q: Doesn't Paul say that prophecy is to be preferred over tongues?

A: No. First Corinthians 14:1 says, "Desire spiritual *gifts,* but especially that you may prophesy." The context of Paul's remarks concerns the conduct of a public worship service as you read the rest of the chapter (see 4:3, 4).

Q: Is it true that not all believers will receive the gift of tongues when they are Holy Spirit baptized?

A: The controversy surrounds 1 Corinthians 12:30, "Do all speak with tongues?" The implied answer of the text is "no." However, there are two issues relevant to this question. One, if Paul is referring to the *public exercise of the gift of tongues* which is to be interpreted for the edification of the congregation, then the answer *is* no, not all people will function in that exercise. Two, if Paul is referring to the *devotional use of spiritual language* then the answer is YES, all believers who have been baptized in the Holy Spirit may speak in tongues.

In reality, however, not all will use their privilege. Paul's remarks in: 1) Romans 8:26—on Holy Spirit assisted intercession, 2) 1 Corinthians 14:2—on the privilege of speaking to God in an unknown tongue, 3) 1 Corinthians 14:4—on personal edification, 4) 1 Corinthians 14:5—on Paul's desire for all to speak in tongues, and 5) 1 Corinthians 4:18—on Paul's personal commitment to the devotional use of tongues, make no sense if God has sovereignly chosen some for this privilege and rejected others.

Q: Aren't all tongues supposed to be interpreted?

A: First Corinthians 14:28 is referring to the public exercise of the gift of tongues, not to the devotional use of tongues.

Q: Aren't all tongues really just foreign languages to be used for evangelism?

A: Read Acts 10:44-46. Who was evangelized by the Gentiles speaking in tongues? Read 1 Corinthians 14:2. Who is being addressed when people speak in tongues in this context?

Q: What does Paul mean in 1 Corinthians 14:15, "I will pray with the spirit . . . I will sing with the spirit."

A: This is prayer and song in a person's spiritual language. For further information, see Lesson 6, "The Song of the Spirit."

Q: Is it wrong for people to praise the Lord in their spiritual language in church services or sing in their spiritual language at the same time? What about 1 Corinthians 14:27?

A: Paul is addressing the conduct of public worship. If there is an endless succession of messages in tongues with or without interpretation, the public meeting will become confusing and cease to edify the body. Clearly in Acts 10:46, the believers all spoke in tongues at the same time, and it was received as praise to God. Paul certainly endorses both prayer and singing with a person's spiritual language.

MINISTRY CHALLENGES TO SPIRITUAL LANGUAGE

Q: Isn't it selfish to edify yourself by speaking in tongues?

A: No. If it is a good thing for the church to be edified by prophecy (1 Cor. 14:4, 5), then it is a good thing for the individual to be edified. However, it is always possible that an insensitive person would exercise his or her personal privilege in a way that might interfere with the rest of the congregation when they gather. Obviously, this should be corrected when it occurs. For further information, see Lesson 2, "The Purpose for Spiritual Language."

Q: Why are some people who speak in tongues so immature in the Lord?

A: The baptism with the Holy Spirit is a gift (Acts 2:38, 10:45). Gifts from God are free, and thereby received by faith without consideration of our personal growth.

Q: Are Spirit-filled believers better Christians?

A: NO. However, a Spirit-filled believer has opened to a realm of supernatural resource by the Holy Spirit for the purpose of expanded ministry to the Body of Christ and outreach to the world (1 Cor. 12:7–31).

Q: Are there such things as false tongues?

A: There are demonic counterfeits to many of the supernatural gifts God has given His church. Of recent date the fascination with New Age healing, prophecy, and knowledge is very pronounced in our culture. Matthew 24:24 warns of "great signs" done by "false christs and false prophets." The imitation of Holy Spirit gifts is not new, read Acts 8:9–11; 13:8.

Q: What if a person says he or she has received the baptism with the Holy Spirit and has yet to speak in tongues?

A: First, do not argue with them. What God begins in a heart may take some time to complete. Second, encourage them to receive everything that is available in the Holy Spirit (1 Cor. 14:5). When people open to the miracle power of the Holy Spirit, it is usually just a matter of time before they begin to speak with tongues.

PERSONAL QUESTIONS ABOUT TONGUES

Q: How can I be sure that I'm not just making up this new language?

A: Luke 11:13 promises that you get from the heavenly Father exactly what you ask for. He does not disappoint His children who seek Him. By faith we receive this gift from the Father. Be confident that He is at work as you have asked.

Q: Why does my language not sound like a language to me?

A: Not all earthly languages sound alike, so why should heavenly languages sound alike? There are fundamental differences in sound between Romance languages and Oriental languages—is one set more authentic than the others? In Africa one of the tribal dialects sounds like a succession of clicking noises to the outsider. But to members of that dialect group, it is a full language. Trust the Holy Spirit, after all, "he who speaks in a tongue does not speak to men but to God" (1 Cor. 14:2).

Q: Why didn't I feel anything special when I received my spiritual language?

A: Personal experience varies widely on receiving the baptism with the Holy Spirit. Just as with salvation, some people have dramatic testimonies of deeply moving emotional experiences when they receive the Lord. Others give their lives to the Lord in a rather sober and unemotional fashion. Some of the differences are personality-based. Some are related to the circumstance in which they occur. Both are completely valid.

Q: Why is it that when I use my spiritual language it does not feel "natural" to me?

A: We do not "learn" our spiritual language—we speak as the Holy Spirit "gives utterance" (Acts 2:4). We do, however, need to learn to allow ourselves to speak this new language without our need to consciously direct our speech patterns in our mother tongue. For some people this takes time and use. Using your spiritual language for fifteen minutes daily during your devotional time will help you become more "fluent" in your spiritual language.

Q: Is it possible that I am simply imitating the spiritual language of the person who prayed for me when I received my spiritual language?

A: This question occurs because some people instruct those they pray for to begin their spiritual language by repeating phrases from their own spiritual language. This sows real doubt in the minds of many who have received their spiritual language this way. When you pray for someone to receive the baptism with the Holy Spirit, trust the Holy Spirit to give them their language from the beginning. If you have these doubts, they are either born of human fear or a devilish lie—once again read Luke 11:9–13. The Father does not allow us to receive a cheap imitation of the real thing!

1. R. C. H. Lenski, *The Interpretation of St. Paul's First and Second Epistles to the Corinthians* (Minneapolis, MN: Augsburg Press, 1963), 563. Henry Alford, *The New Testament for English Readers*, Vol. 3 (Grand Rapids, MI: Baker Book House, 1983), 1058. W. Robertson Nicoll, *The Expositor's Greek Testament*, Vol. 2 (Grand Rapids, MI: William B. Eerdmans Publishing Company, 1990), 900. F. W. Grosheide, *Commentary on the First Epistle to the Corinthians*, The New International Commentary on the New Testament, (Grand Rapids, MI: William B. Eerdmans Publishing Company, 1980), 309. F. F. Bruce, *First and Second Corinthians*, New Century Bible (Greenwood, SC: Attic Press, 1976), 128. Saint Chrysostom, *Homilies on the Epistle of Paul to the Corinthians; Nicene and Post-Nicene Fathers of the Christian Church*, ed. Philip Schaff (Grand Rapids, MI: William B. Eerdmans Publishing Company, 1969), 202.

Epilogue: The Giver's and Receiver's Hearts

THE HEART OF THE GIVER

We've spent ample time now going over the biblical foundation of spiritual language and reviewing the many aspects of how it applies to the life of the believer. But the primary objective in spiritual language is not complicated or difficult to comprehend. It is simply seen in the heart of the Father toward us: He wants His children to be able to communicate with Him, and He longs to reveal Himself to them.

Look up the following Scriptures. Write down how God's love is described and how the baptism with the Holy Spirit helps us to receive His love, communicate with Him, and understand His nature.

Romans 5:8

1 Corinthians 2:9, 10

1 Corinthians 14:2

Galatians 4:6

Ephesians 1:17

Ephesians 2:18

Ephesians 3:14, 17–19

Colossians 1:26, 27

1 John 3:1

Scripture reveals Jesus as an expression of the heart of the Father (John 10:30; 14:9). Look up the following verses and write down what Jesus' attitude toward Holy Spirit baptism was.

Matthew 3:11

Mark 16:17

Luke 24:49

Acts 1:4, 5

What does Luke 24:49 reveal about why Jesus was so interested in His disciples receiving the baptism with the Holy Spirit?

What was the "power" Jesus promised to be used for (Acts 1:8)?

THE HEART OF THE RECEIVER

As we look at the Father's love for us and Jesus' desire to see His disciples baptized with the Holy Spirit, we see that the baptism with the Holy Spirit and the attendant spiritual language is given to us so that we can communicate with the Father beyond our human limitations (Rom. 8:26) and so that we can be resourced for service (Acts 1:8).

That leaves us with the simple question: What is our heart toward the baptism with the Holy Spirit supposed to be? First, we need to know who is offering the gift. Look again at Matthew 3:11. Who was John the Baptist talking about in saying "He will baptize you with the Holy Spirit"?

What word is used in Acts 2:38 to describe the baptism with the Holy Spirit?

If, then, we *know* the One who wants to baptize us with the Holy Spirit, and that baptism is described as a *gift,* our hearts should be open and ready to receive what He desires to give us. Look up the following verses that tell us about the gifts God has for us. Write down how they describe God's gifts.

Luke 11:13

John 4:10 (compare with John 7:37–39)

Romans 5:18

2 Corinthians 9:15

Ephesians 2:8

2 Timothy 1:6, 7

Hebrews 2:3, 4

James 1:17

1 Peter 4:10

Finally, look up and write out the verses that define what the apostle Paul says our attitude toward spiritual language is to be.

1 Corinthians 14:5

1 Corinthians 14:18

1 Corinthians 14:39